beneath a tall tree
a story about us

jean strauss

ARETÉ

PUBLISHING
USA

beneath a tall tree
a story about us

jean strauss

ARETÉ

PUBLISHING
USA

A Rose/Skye Imprint

Arete Publishing Company of America
a Rose/Skye imprint

P.O. Box 127, Claremont, California 91711 U.S.A.

www.arete-usa.com

LIBRARY OF CONGRESS CATALOGING IN PUBLICATION DATE

Beneath a Tall Tree/ Jean A. S. Strauss.

1. Jean A. S. Strauss, date. 2. Narrative Memoir. 3. Genealogy.
I. Strauss, Jean A. S. II. Title.

ISBN: 0-9627982-0-7

Printed in the United States of America

Cover by Cinnamon Design.
Claremont, California

dedicated to

Mary
and all who came before

Tiff and Jonathon
and all who follow

and Jon
because now is now

... for every atom belonging to me
as good belongs to you....

Walt Whitman
"Song of Myself"

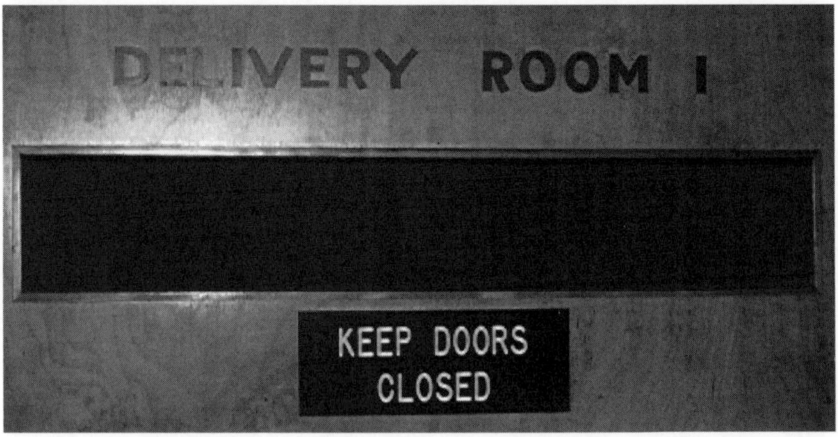
DELIVERY ROOM I
KEEP DOORS
CLOSED

1955

The young woman stares out the hospital window at the rolling green hills and the California poppies, like gold in the morning sun. She has never seen an uglier day.

A nurse has packed her things for her as if she is a child instead of a twenty-year-old secretary at the FBI. Her toothbrush, her nightgown, and her other clothes sit in a bag on her lap as the wheelchair is pushed through the corridor. People tower above her, the chair making her feel as if she is beneath everyone.

The orderly pushing the chair never says a word, even when he deposits her at the desk in the yellow-walled lobby. They are waiting there for her, the social worker and the baby. She knows better than to think of it as her baby. She knows she has no right to think such a thing. Outside of committing murder, there isn't much a girl could do that is worse than getting pregnant.

"I have one last release form you need to sign," the social worker in the gray suit says.

The young woman takes the paper, pretending to read it. She could read before she even went to kindergarten, but right now her eyes don't seem to work. Everything is blurry. She looks at the baby girl asleep in the social worker's arms. "I want to do the right thing," she says in the same tone of voice she uses in the confessional at Church.

"Giving the baby to a loving family is the right thing." The social worker's voice is soothing. "For both of you."

The young woman stares at the form, all it's blanks filled in, except for the place where she is to write her name. She knows if she signs this piece of paper, people might forgive her. Maybe even her parents.

Why hadn't anyone told her how she'd feel after the baby was born? These last three days she'd been overwhelmed by instincts to protect and nurture her child. Nothing inside prepared her for this moment right now.

Is this how her own mother felt twenty years ago, the mother she is not supposed to think about or mention, the one who gave her away, is she just like her? By getting pregnant out of wedlock, does she now know her own mother for the first time?

"The burden of illegitimacy is unfair for any child." The social worker says this as if reciting the words from a textbook.

The young woman nods. She understands. Being a good mother requires a gold band on the ring finger of her left hand. She does not have this equipment. She presses the pen against the form. Tears fall and the ink of her signature runs.

"Can I give you a lift?"

She is surprised at the social worker's offer. She has not thought about how she will get back to the house where she has hidden away these last weeks. She has not thought about what she will do the rest of the day. Or the rest of her life.

When they reach the car in the hospital parking lot, the social worker begins to place the baby in a basket on the back seat. "May I hold her?" the young woman asks, and the baby is placed in her arms, opening her wide blue eyes and staring at the young woman's face. The young woman stares back, memorizing Cecilia. She gave the baby this name after the patron saint of music, and because Cecilia is her own middle name, the name given her by that shadowy stranger, her own mother, the other one, the unspoken one, the ghost. The name Cecilia Anne is the only gift she can give to her daughter.

The drive is short, too short. The social worker steers the car parallel to the curb and shifts into park. She does not turn off the engine. Nothing is said. The idle of the motor says it all: it is time.

The young woman averts her eyes from the baby, from everything but the window. "She'll hate me, won't she."

"She'll know you cared enough about her to give her to people who will love her."

The young woman wants to shout, "What about me? I love her!" But she says nothing as the social worker takes Cecilia from her arms and places her in the basket on the back seat. In an odd gesture of finality, the social worker pulls a flannel blanket up over the baby's face. It is sudden and unexpected. Cecilia is gone.

This is like death, the young woman realizes, as if a casket is being sealed, covering up all trace of her daughter. But she cannot change her mind. Papers have been signed, all legal claim forfeited. A voice inside her whispers, "Take the baby and run!" Instead she asks the questions again. They are like a prayer. "You have a family for her? That'll baptize her? And her name. They'll keep her name?"

The social worker gives the same answers. "Yes. I'm taking the baby to her new family today, a good Catholic home. And they'll keep her name, I promise." The social worker doesn't mean to lie. She means to make this easier.

The car door scrapes open against the curb. With a last look back at the baby she can no longer see, the young woman slides out and closes the door. Cecilia begins to cry and the young mother stands motionless at the curb, listening to her baby, the baby, crying, as the car pulls away. She watches the taillights of the car disappear around the corner. And her daughter is gone.

She cannot move at first, nor does she feel anything. The event is too large to grasp, her emotions replaced by an absence of feeling, a numbness, like the first instant after a knife cut and there is no pain.

She crosses the street to the house where she has lived, an outcast. The people who live there, friends of her parents, had not come to the hospital. No one had come. She sits alone on the front stoop looking out into the empty street. She has her life back. People have told her this is what she wants, what she needs. They were wrong.

She felt like a criminal when she learned she was pregnant. But she knows in her heart she's never done anything criminal in her life - until now. A stranger has just driven away with her baby. The young woman wraps her arms around her knees, rocking back and forth, as milk falls from her breasts, like tears.

earth

My Family Tree

■ ←————— this is me

1

I am three years old. My father carries me in his arms through the lath house where newly-watered geraniums hang from the roof dripping upon us, like rain. He unlatches the gate and strides out the pathway behind our home.

His name is Lou. It used to be Luigi, but he changed it long ago. The son of Italian immigrants, he has worked hard to prove that he is an American. We live in a custom ranch house on a country lane east of San Francisco, with redwoods protecting us from the sun and wind.

My father smells of pipe tobacco and wears a loose flannel shirt and baggy khaki pants. He is Vince Lombardi's twin, or would be if Vince Lombardi had a twin. I wrap my arms around his neck as the path ends and his brown canvas shoes make their way through clods of newly rototilled earth.

He reaches the crest of the hill and stops, facing west. The summer air is dry and a fan of white cirrus clouds sweep across the horizon. I examine the pattern of his flannel shirt, brown on yellow on white, my fingers trace the lines. Then the sun slides behind La Cañada ridge, and my father grins, pointing. I look up. An orange-pink light bounces off the bottom of the clouds and my father's face glows in a golden light. It is magic. It is my earliest memory.

I can close my eyes and see this moment clearly even now, almost a half century later. I can smell the California adobe and the oat hay and wild mustard. I can feel the skin of my father's cheek against mine, sandpaper rough, a man's skin at dusk.

I remember many things from childhood. I remember Miss Nelson's Nursery School graduation, receiving a diploma with Kleenex packed in my bloody nose. Very pug. I remember starting kindergarten, the smell of the white paste and the pride I felt to see my name taped to the table where I was to sit. I remember the disappointment I felt when I entered first grade and learned we had to use fat black crayons to write with rather than fountain pens. That same year I read my first novel, *The Little Red Book,* with Dick and Jane and Spot providing absolutely riveting material despite the lack of any antagonist or plot. At Christmas I received a Betsy Wetsy doll. I had asked for a horse. Betsy was later given a hair cut and used for target practice by the neighborhood boys during a dirt clod war, an abuse I not only applauded, but participated in.

I remember every one of my teachers; the day I learned to ride a bike; watching John Glenn blast off in Friendship 7; running home in tears when a boy on the school bus told me President Kennedy was dead. I remember this and much more.

But I do not remember when I was first told I was adopted. It was one of the most important things my parents ever told me. It explained how I became their child and how I got my name, Jean Anne Sacconaghi. It explained everything. They first told me when I was three-years-old while reading me a story about an adoptive family, but I have no memory of the moment at all.

The only thing I can remember is the reflection of the sunset in my father's eyes.

2

I am not a brave child.

I stand beneath a tall tree and watch as the neighborhood kids climb the steps nailed into the side of the huge Eucalyptus and disappear into the plywood fort twenty feet above. Their faces peer over the edge as they look down at me, four-years-old, my feet planted firmly on the earth below. "Come on up!"

But I am afraid to follow, afraid of being so high. Their faces disappear and I hear giggling. Such abandonment is difficult to bear. I lean my face into the tree's thick trunk, my nose against the peeling skin-like bark, and begin to cry.

The tree stops me. I forget all about the children laughing above and take a deep breath, inhaling the aroma of Eucalyptus. I reach down and pick up a handful of the feather-shaped leaves and press them to my face. They smell just like Vicks Vaporub, the stuff Mom uses when I have a cold. I smile.

Mom, who everyone else calls Betty, is my ally against all hurts. She reaches her arm protectively across me every time she uses the brakes in our old Dodge station wagon. She lifts me up onto the kitchen counter to put Bactine and Band-Aids on my scraped knees. I don't like being apart from her. My very first sentence was, "Mommy, where are you?"

There is another woman she tells me about sometimes, the one who gave birth to me, but I do not think of *her* as my mother. No, Mom is the one who makes nightmares melt with a spoonful of brown sugar in the dark night. She is home every day in the house down the hill with the braided rugs and the knotted-pine ceilings. She is there right now.

I am wearing my brand new navy blue Keds, the shoes that make kids run faster and jump higher. I see children in my mind, boys and girls in hues of grey, airborne in slow motion with their Keds, images absorbed from our RCA television set which has twelve whole channels, from two to thirteen.

It is downhill all the way. I soar home, flying down La Cañada hill just like the kids on television, making huge leaping bounds in my Keds, the fistful of Eucalyptus leaves gripped tight in my hand.

Mom is there, just like I knew she would be, with unfiltered Camels and coffee with cream, sitting at the table in the family room with her two best friends, Lue and Margaret. The housework is done for the day. Now it is their time.

Our formal dining table is actually a round outdoor picnic table made of redwood, with a hole in the center for an umbrella and curved benches to sit on. My parents are saving up for a real dining room set made of maple. They do not buy on credit.

I don't tell Mom about the Eucalyptus tree or that the ad about Keds is right, they really do make me jump higher. Instead, I crawl to my favorite spot underneath the table where I can observe the three of them through the umbrella hole. The hole becomes whatever I want it to be. It is a telescope. Or a magnifying glass.

I lie back on the carpet and listen to their laughter and talk, the sound of their voices overlapping, like water running over stones. Listening to them, I feel connected to everything there ever was and everything there ever will be. I lie there smelling the leaves I clutch in my fist and pretend that I am twenty feet off the ground.

3

My brother Frankie was adopted from an agency far away in Los Angeles. A year-and-a-half older than me, they got him first. He reminds me of this often. "They'll take you back before me," he says, knowing this will scare me. He likes to scare me.

On New Year's Eve, Mom and Dad go out on a rare date, hiring the boy up the street to babysit us. "Remember, the sitter's in charge while we're gone," Mom says as Dad helps her into her coat. "Do as he says."

The minute they leave, Frankie instructs the sitter, "I get to stay up later than *her* because I'm older."

The babysitter leans back and puts his feet up on the coffee table, something my parents tell us we are not supposed to do. "I'm the oldest in my family, too," he says, glancing at me.

Frankie smiles. A comrade. "Can I stay up until midnight?"

"Sure," the sitter grins. "As long as you don't tell your folks."

"I'll tell," I say.

"No you won't." Frankie looks at me. "It's time for you to go to bed."

"I don't want to go to bed."

"Read her a story," Frankie says. "They always read her a story." He picks out a slim bound Golden Book and hands it to the sitter.

I see that it's *Hansel and Gretel.* "No! I hate that one."

The sitter shrugs. "Then it's straight to bed."

"Okay." I don't like how this is going at all. We sit on the couch, me in my pajamas, Frankie still in his play clothes, as the sitter starts to read. When Hansel and Gretel get lost in the forest, I cover my ears. The notion of being lost in the dark woods terrifies me. I think about birds eating the bread crumbs, and I worry: what if the children can't find their way home?

"Chicken," Frankie says, kicking my bare foot with his hard shoe.

"Ow!"

The children continue deeper into the forest, finally reaching the witch's house. Our babysitter gets to the part I hate most: the part about the witch and the oven. Frankie interrupts him. "Nobody could fit into an oven."

"Yes they could," says the sitter. "This was written over a hundred years ago, and ovens were like..." He pauses, searching for a good example.

"Like our barbeque pit?" asks Frankie.

In our family room is a custom-made barbeque pit built right into the brick wall. At least once a week Dad cooks dinner there, his tall chef's hat at an angle on his head, an apron tied around his waist, a flank steak on the grill. Frankie looks at me and smiles. "Let's see if a little kid would really fit in there."

Suddenly I feel myself being hoisted by the sitter off the couch into the barbeque pit. "No!" I scream in terror. "Stop!" But I am trapped, the sitter playfully boxing me in as Frankie gleefully seasons me with the long handled salt and pepper shakers. They howl with laughter as if this is the funniest thing they have ever seen.

For weeks, Mom and Dad are awakened nightly by my screams. Invariably, the story is the same. "I was being chased by a witch and she shoved me into the barbeque pit!"

Mom never hires the same babysitter again, but the babysitter isn't the problem. During a pillow fight, my brother sits on my chest, pressing a pillow against my face. I struggle, panicked at how difficult it is to breathe, but he will not let go, suffocating me until Dad hears my muffled screams and pulls him off.

We watch *The Wizard of Oz* on the black and white RCA and the story is even scarier than Hansel and Gretel. There are tornados and witches and feet that shrivel up under a house. When monkeys swoop down from the sky and take Dorothy away, Frankie points out the window and shouts, "Look! Flying monkeys, coming for you!" I run to my room and hide and don't see the end of the film until a whole year later when I am five.

The death of the Wicked Witch of the West is even more nightmarish than the flying monkeys. Frankie throws a bucket of water on me in the back yard and yells, "You're melting!" He spends hours in his room for this offense. He doesn't care.

He takes my most prized possessions, plastic horses that stand a foot high, and uses them for target practice with his b-b gun. 'Zip, zip', the b-b's ricochet off the plastic, leaving pock marks on the horses' sides. My favorite, a big bay stallion in a rearing pose, falls over backward, shattering one of his legs. Frankie is spanked this time.

He sees me alone in the school hallway. Bam! His fist connects with my arm. "Stop!" I say, trying to escape, but he grabs my wrist. "I'm going to tell."

He shoves me against the wall. "No you won't."

But of course I'll tell. I always tell. I relish the moments when he sins, because I know he will pay for them. "Try and stop me," I say. Am I being brave or provoking him?

He grabs my hair and pulls hard.

"Ow!" This really does hurt and I begin to cry.

"Frankie!" Mr. Barbieri's stern voice reverberates down the hallway.

I grimace for effect. My brother has been caught, by the school principal no less. It is worth taking a hundred punches to see the reaction on his face. He is dead meat. But at the last moment I reach out and tug on Mr. Barbieri's hand until he kneels down beside me. "Don't hurt him," I plead.

The principal's huge hand pats my blond hair. I have achieved sainthood. My brother is led down the hall by his arm, struggling angrily in Mr. Barbieri's grip. I stand watching them, hoping Mr. Barbieri doesn't really do anything to my brother. All I want him to do is call home and report Frankie to our parents.

"What did he do now?" my mother will sigh and she will tell my father when he comes home from work. They will talk in low voices behind the closed door of their bedroom and I will hear their confusion and their concern about protecting me as I listen with my ear at their door. Neither of them ever says, "If he doesn't begin to behave, we're taking him back to that adoption agency." No adult in our house has ever threatened such a thing. The notion of one of us being 'returned' is only a taunt my brother uses to scare me. I know deep down that such a thing would never happen.

But even so, every time Frankie gets in trouble, I heave a sigh of relief. It makes me worry less that they got him first. It makes me less concerned that he's the oldest and there are twice as many baby pictures of him in the family photo album. When he hits me, I relax. It's insurance. It makes me feel positive that if they ever *do* decide to return one of us, it'll be Frankie, not me.

4

Everyone in the second grade has a last name like Johnson or Keeling or Hoover or Perry. Everyone except me. I am different. I am a Sacconaghi. Sometimes I like how grownups stumble over my last name and look twice. They do not expect me to have blond hair and blue eyes. "Your last name sounds Oriental," they say, and I like how the name makes them pay attention to me.

But other times I don't like being different. I wish my name was not so foreign, but I cannot help what it is. My grandparents were not born in America but in northern Italy, and so we are Sacconaghi's, people with a last name that everyone says sounds Japanese.

Not only does my grandparents' last name make me feel I don't quite belong, sometimes even my grandparents make me feel that way, too. I see them once a year when we make the nine hour drive down the El Camino Real, past fields of artichokes and garlic, to their house in Santa Barbara. The air on De La Guerra Street smells of orange blossoms and roses and my grandparents' yard is beautifully landscaped. Grandpa is a renowned gardener. In Santa Barbara, he is known as the 'Chrysanthemum King'.

Whenever we visit, I never seem to do the right thing. Part of it has to do with not understanding the delicate nature of flowers. Running through their yard, I step where I shouldn't. "Look what you did!" Grandpa growls. He bends down, touching the broken stem of a plant, and I know by his look that the plant is more important than me.

"Sorry Grandpa." He is silent as he gently pulls the plant from the earth and cradles it in his rough hands.

I move to the front steps, trying to sit still, running my hands across the terra cotta surface of the stairs until my palms turn red. Then I paint my cheeks to look like an Indian in war paint. Davy Crockett on NBC would be proud.

Mom scowls when she sees me. "Look at you." She doesn't ever seem to mind me being dirty at home, but in Santa Barbara I need to be someone different. "Go change," she says, then softens. "Wash your hands and face."

Inside the breeze way is my favorite thing: a water cooler. I fill one of the paper cones, watching bubbles gurgle to the top of the bottle. I drink the water and fill the cup again. Frankie pushes me aside and grabs a cup. We fight over who gets to push the blue button.

"It's my turn!" he shouts. More bubbles rise to the surface as water spills on the floor.

I hear Grandma Sacconaghi in the kitchen. "Tsk, tsk."

Mom's shoes click across the linoleum. "That's not a toy," she scolds. "Go get cleaned up for dinner."

My grandparents' home smells of mothballs and old lace and in the living room the skin of a coyote, head and all, hangs over their fireplace screen, its jaw permanently set in a savage pose. I think it's a wolf, and no one corrects me. Grandpa tells me he shot off part of his finger killing it. Once, he let me touch the stub of his index finger.

"Where is it now?" I ask.

"What?"

"The rest of your finger."

"Gone," says Grandpa gruffly, pulling back his hand.

I make a wide arc to avoid the fireplace, afraid the wolf might somehow spring to life, snapping its fangs upon me, and return to the kitchen smelling of Lifebuoy soap, my face scrubbed clean of terra cotta rouge. Grandma Sacconaghi pinches my cheeks, almost lifting me off the ground.

She is nothing like the grandmothers I see on television. She speaks broken English and never bakes chocolate chip cookies. Instead she makes polenta, one of my father's favorite foods.

Polenta is an Italian dish made of coarse cornmeal. I loath it. Squirming on the rigid wooden chair in the dining room, my elbows on the off-white table cloth, I push the polenta around on my plate, trying to make it appear as if I have tried some, as is our family rule. I hear my father clearing his throat and look up. Across the table I meet his embarrassed eyes. He doesn't say a word, but his disappointment in me is clear. I sigh heavily, dramatically holding my nose as I put a forkful of polenta into my mouth and swallow. My father grips his fork tightly, shifting his eyes down to his plate.

His shame in my behavior is not lost on my grandmother who watches silently from her chair, her head shaking imperceptibly from side to side. There is something in her gesture that makes me know real grandchildren would not act this way.

She was born across the Atlantic in a house that had a dirt floor and no indoor plumbing. To her, family is something you are born into not something you are invited to join. I am a post-World War II baby-boomer, born to strangers, yet given a life of privilege with a roof over my head and a hardwood floor under my feet. My grandmother's eyes slide past me to the empty spaces where there are no chairs, as if trying to see the other children who should be there at the table, the real ones, the ones who were never born.

I know I have made a fatal mistake by whining about her best polenta. I will show her. I will prove to her that I am as good as any empty space. I take another bite, tears in my eyes, wishing I could spit the yellow paste from my mouth, yet all the while wondering: if I *was* real, would the polenta taste any better?

5

"Today we're going to make a family tree," says Mrs. Stadleman, my third grade teacher, passing out large sheets of blank manila paper. "A family tree is a chart of your ancestors. Does anyone know what an ancestor is?"

Hands shoot up. "Your grandparents!"

"And their parents!"

"Dead people!"

Mrs. Stadleman smiles stiffly. "Your ancestors are the family you were born into. From them you inherit everything that you are."

I always brag about my adoption status on the school playground. "My parents *chose* me," I tell everyone. "That makes me special." But what Mrs. Stadleman says right now makes my stomach hurt.

"Your parents gave birth to you," she explains, "just like their parents gave birth to them, and so on, and so on, back through the generations. They are the people who made you who you are. They are your family tree."

I sink in my chair, realizing.

"I know most of you know your grandparents," Mrs. Stadleman continues, "but do any of you know your great grandparents?"

Again hands wave in the air. I sit on mine. I feel an emptiness inside, a black hole. Who are my ancestors? Mrs. Stadleman is still talking but I no longer hear her. A second question floats to the surface, like a dead body. Where did I come from? I look around me and feel slightly dizzy, as if the room is not quite level.

There is a lot of noise. Everyone is talking all at once. The third grade is rarely quiet. For that matter, I am rarely quiet. But right now I can't speak, all I can do is hear. Everyone seems to know something about where they came from. One girl, who knows her ancestors all the way back to the time of the Revolutionary War, is talking about something called the DAR. One of the boys is related to Abraham Lincoln.

"What if you don't know where you came from?" I whisper to the girl in front of me.

"Everybody knows that," she whispers back. "Unless you're stupid."

That explains it. Family trees are a reflection of intelligence. I sit in the second to last row, frowning at the paper in front of me, its edges seeming to extend past the surface of my desk, spilling over onto the floor, its blankness overwhelming. I take the point of my pencil and make a small speck in the center. This is me.

A shadow falls across the page and Mrs. Stadleman peers like a giant over my shoulder. She is very nice but has a streak of white hair that makes her look somewhat like the wicked stepmother in Disney's *Cinderella*. "Well my fine-feathered friend," she says. This is how Mrs. Stadleman addresses each one of us in her class. "Are you having trouble getting started?"

"I'm adopted," I blurt out.

"Oh."

"I don't have any ancestors."

Mrs. Stadleman does a lateral pass. "Why don't you take your family tree home and discuss it with your parents."

For some reason, taking that blank piece of paper home and talking to Mom and Dad about it is the last thing I want to do. "It's okay," I say, smiling as convincingly as possible. "I can do it."

As she nods and moves on, I exhale. I put my name in the center at the bottom of the sheet, then use my ruler to make lines for Frankie and my parents and my grandparents and my aunts and uncles and cousins, just like Mrs. Stadleman has drawn on the blackboard. I lean down close to the paper, hiding my work, my pencil moving carefully, as if I am forging a signature.

Questions spin in my mind. Who are the people I came from? What do they look like? Do they love horses? Do they hate polenta? Why did they give me away? I think about Hansel and Gretel and bread crumbs scattered on the forest floor and I decide: someday I will find out where I came from.

When I finish my work, I look at my manila family tree and feel as if I have just told a lie. Mrs. Stadleman puts a gold star sticker upon it, commenting on the unusual neatness of my handwriting. I always take such masterpieces home, but not today. At the dismissal bell, I dart into the girls bathroom and crumple up my family tree, stuffing it into the white metal trash can by the sink.

It's not that I don't want to see my parents and grandparents on the chart with me, it's that I don't want to think about what the family tree means. Even more important, I don't want my parents to think about what it means.

I bury the tree deep inside the trash can before racing out to catch the school bus and go home.

6

Grandma Sacconaghi dies of a heart attack right after Christmas. Months later, when we watch the home movies taken at our house just eleven days before she died, I notice something I never let myself see before: Grandma Sacconaghi had the most lovely smile. It just lit up the room. And during a moment on camera she turned and smiled at me. Right at *me*. It is my best memory of her, captured on a piece of celluloid that I don't see until after she is gone.

Grandpa decides to sell the house on De La Guerra Street and move into ours on La Cañada Road, four hundred miles away. My parents design an addition for our house, a bedroom with a private bath and brick steps that lead out to the garden in the backyard.

It is exciting. I watch the carpenters as they work on, collecting the leftover junction-box knock-out plugs, pretending they are nickels. When Grandpa arrives, he and Dad build a hothouse for his prize orchids. Our gentle hillside turns into a show-place full of roses and snapdragons. Thriving vegetable beds border our property line and the branches of our apricot and plum trees sag under the weight of their crops.

Grandpa rises daily before dawn and sits on an old metal folding chair in the backyard, his ancient shotgun (the same one which accidentally shot off his finger) lying across his lap, ready to ward off any deer or raccoon that attempt to devour his plants.

Frankie and I make money during summer vacation peddling his fresh vegetables door to door. A quarter for a sack of foot long cucumbers. Fifty cents for a dozen ears of golden corn. There is no doubt our grandfather is a magician with plants. Children are another matter.

I have an image in my mind of the relationship I want to have with Grandpa, one exactly like what Beaver Cleaver has with Gus the Fireman on

Leave It To Beaver. I am seeking a wise mentor in my grandfather. I follow him around the yard, talking non-stop. "What are you doing Grandpa?"

He stirs the earth beneath a rosebush with his trowel.

"Can I help?"

He makes a ridged circle of soil at the base of the plant.

"In school today we learned about barometers. Do you know about them?"

He turns on the hose, the water not too fast, not too slow and I watch as he gently fills the moat of earth he has formed.

"Can I do that?"

Ours is a very one-sided conversation. Grandpa prefers silence. He prefers things with roots in the soil. "Grandpa, how come the roses don't die when you cut off their branches like that?"

He shrugs.

"What's all that yellow and blue stuff you put on ground?"

He must not have heard me, as he gently holds a rose by its stem, careful not to touch its bloom, searching for signs of aphids.

I never ask him, "How come you don't like me as much as you like flowers?" I know the answer. Frankie and I are adopted. He tries to love us, because he loves his son, but he doesn't know how to graft us together, like he does hybrid varieties of orchids.

My vision of a 'Gus the Fireman' relationship with Grandpa gradually goes away. I am puzzled that relationships aren't as easy as the ones I see on television. I sense that certain things work against us, not only my lack of family blood, but the fact that I am a girl.

Three generations of men live in our house, and they share a certain fraternity. They fish. They leave on their expeditions before dawn, returning when the sun is high in the sky, dirty and smelling like moss, standing side-by-side in the kitchen, cleaning their catches in the sink. I want to be a member of their club. "Why can't I go?"

"Girls don't fish, honey." Dad is perplexed by my desire. But when we spend a week at a family camp in the Sierra foothills, Mom insists he *has* to take me. The morning I am to go, Dad and Grandpa toss a coin to see who 'gets' me. Dad wins. That means I go with Grandpa.

Frankie follows Dad to a little cove on the Feather River, while Grandpa and I make our way across stones at a shallow spot and plant ourselves on the opposite bank. The damp soil feels good beneath me and I smile at Grandpa as he prepares his gear, then baits my hook with a red salmon egg. Without a word he casts out both our lines.

I watch his every move, afraid to breathe lest I risk banishment. When Grandpa catches a rainbow trout, it is the first time I've ever seen a fish reeled in. I take note of how he plays the fish, how he doesn't make any sharp movements. Removing the hook, he stows the wiggling fish in his creel and recasts his line. I mimic his every move, patiently clicking in my line and check my bait. After two tries, I cast my own line out into the stream, then sit down on the sandy bank and take a deep breath of the cool air and nod my head, just like my grandfather nods his. I never say a word, because fishermen obviously never talk. It is just the two of us and the river and the rising sun and the nylon line and the tip of the pole that will jerk ever so slightly when a fish has taken the bait.

Prokofiev's "Peter and the Wolf" theme would have been appropriate to accompany our return to camp midday. Dad and Frankie arrive without having caught a single fish. Grandpa's rainbow trout pokes it's nose stiffly out of his creel. He has to help me carry mine; the one with nine trout in it.

I never have to beg to be taken fishing again. The following year on my birthday, Dad gives me my very own light green fiberglass rod and with a shiny spin reel and Grandpa ruffles my hair and smiles when I show it to him. It is the moment I know: I belong.

7

Mrs. Webb wears horn-rimmed glasses and displays a gap between her front teeth whenever she smiles, which is often. She is my most favorite person in the whole world outside of my family, and I am sure she feels the same way about me.

"Jeannie is very enthusiastic about her studies," she writes on my fourth grade report card in the fall, "but sometimes this gets her into trouble by being too talkative in class." I am sure this just means Mrs. Webb is very fond of me.

I love to read. My favorite book is Laura Ingalls Wilder's <u>Little House in the Big Woods</u>. *"Once upon a time... a little girl lived in the Big Woods of Wisconsin, in a little gray house made of logs."* Reading by flashlight under the covers of my bed, I am there in the cabin in the Big Woods with Ma and Pa and Laura and Mary. I can hear the wolves howling in the night and see the pig bladder they use to play ball and taste the sugar snow and smell the hickory smoke curing bacon.

In fourth grade we get to study the California Missions and I think Father Junipero Serra is right up there with the Ringo Starr. When Mrs. Webb announces that we get to do a report about an individual Mission, I know exactly the one I will pick: Mission Santa Barbara, only a mile from where my dad was born and raised. It is mine.

In addition to writing a report, we are to make a model of our Mission. "I'm going to make tiny adobe bricks," I tell Mrs. Webb, "and build an exact replica of Santa Barbara." She smiles at me with her gap between her two front teeth.

When I arrive home from school and tell Mom my plan, she immediately discourages me. "I think Styrofoam would be easier than making real bricks."

But I want to make an exact replica. "Dad will help me," I say.

Mom gives me a look, a look without words which says I can't ask my father to go outside and dig in the dirt to make a thousand miniature adobe bricks. Dad has been sick for months, so sick he doesn't even go to work anymore. It has something to do with his heart.

"Can we drive to Santa Barbara then?" I ask. "There aren't any books in the library that have pictures of the Mission in them."

"You know we can't."

I sigh, then spend the afternoon making bricks out of mud in our backyard. But the next day when I come home from school, I find they've all cracked apart after baking in the sun. "I've changed my mind," I tell Mom. "I want to carve my Mission out of soap."

"Why don't I pick up some Styrofoam."

"No, I want to carve it." The idea of using a knife sounds particularly exciting. Mom brings home a package of four bars of Ivory Soap from the grocery store, but hard as I try, I can't make those bars into anything except shredded rectangles with holes in them. "I hate this!" I shout in frustration when the last bar splits into pieces.

Mom puts me in the bathtub with the pieces of soap, and my Mission disaster becomes an armada of Franciscan friars sailing across the ocean to settle in California. "Why don't you try Styrofoam," Mom suggests after my fleet melts away in the bath and my hands are wrinkled like raisins.

"No thanks," I say, then add, "Susie's parents are taking her to see Mission Solano. I wish we could go see Santa Barbara." Mom gives me another one of her silent looks and I don't say anything else, but that night, as I am falling asleep, I say my wish to go to Santa Barbara over and over, like a mantra.

Sugar cubes are next. I stack dozens of sugar cubes in perfect rows, only to have them collapse. I don't wait for Mom to make any further suggestions. I poke my head into my parents' bedroom. "Dad, will you help me build my Mission out of Styrofoam?"

He grins his Vince Lombardi grin. "Sure." Together, we cut the walls and arched windows out of the thick block of Styrofoam that Mom had bought without my asking. We use toothpicks to hold the sides together and glue the walls to a thin piece of plywood and make a roof out of cardboard that I paint red. Finally, I use brown and green and blue paint on the plywood base to show the pathways and the farming areas and the aqueduct.

My model doesn't look like the perfect miniature Mission I'd envisioned. When I put it on the counter alongside everyone else's, Mrs. Webb smiles, but she doesn't say it is the best model of a Mission she's ever seen as I had hoped she would.

All that's left is my written report. Dad says, "I know a lot about the Mission." He has to go to the hospital for some tests, but promises to help me on Monday when he gets home.

"What I really wish is that I could go see it," I hint one more time, even though I've given up hope of ever seeing Santa Barbara again.

"I wish you could see it, too," Dad says with a wink, and a glimmer of hope grows within me that maybe my wish will come true.

I spend Sunday riding bikes at a friend's house. Mom is supposed to pick me up late in the afternoon, but she makes arrangements for me to stay for dinner and doesn't come to pick me up until after nine. She barely says a word as we approach our house and I see there are a number of cars parked in our driveway. "Are we having a party?"

Before I can even say hello to anyone inside, Mom gently leads me into the hallway by my bedroom and kneels down, her eyes straight across from mine. "You know your dad has been very sick."

I nod. "He's going to help me finish my Mission report tomorrow."

Mom never moves her eyes from mine. "Jeannie, your father died this morning."

The walls of the hallway shrink in around us. "What?"

"I'm so sorry."

A strange sensation floods through me, as if I am falling, even though I am standing still. Mom's arms encircle me as I begin to cry. And then I ask *the* question. "Are you going to get married again?"

Mom flinches, as if I hit her. "I don't know." I see it in her eyes: how could I ask such a thing? Do I think my father could be so easily replaced? We slip away from each other into the arms of friends and neighbors in the living room. They have brought us casseroles and cakes, even though we are not hungry. I steal glances at Mom across the room. She doesn't understand. She has to get married again. Soon! They've always told me that the woman who gave birth to me couldn't keep me because she wasn't married. If someone at the adoption agency finds out Mom isn't married anymore, they might come and take me away.

Around midnight, Mom tells Frankie and me to get ready for bed. Grandpa intercepts us in the hallway. He has sat silently in the rocking chair by the living room window all evening, but he speaks now, his eyes cold. "It was your fault."

I hear my brother suck in a breath.

"You were such bad kids. You made him too upset, always fighting."

I know what he's talking about. Last weekend, Frankie and I had fought in the backyard and Dad had to come outside in his yellow bathrobe to scold us. What had we done?

"It was your fault," Grandpa says again, pushing past us to his room. My brother and I look at each other. This horrible truth will be our secret.

I lie in bed, unable to sleep. My father is dead because we made him too upset, and because of something else, something my brother and grandfather don't even know about: my wish. For two weeks all I've wished for is to go to Santa Barbara. Now I'll be going there on Wednesday to bury my father. Somehow I have caused this. Between fighting with my brother and wishing to see the Mission, I have made my father die. And I am sure of one thing: if my parents had been able to have their own children, he would still be alive.

We sit in the front row at the funeral service, the open casket before us, my father lying inside without his glasses on, as if he is asleep. So many people come they can't all fit inside the chapel. They file in a long line slowly past his body. I avoid their eyes. I can't face that I have wished us to this place.

Before we leave Santa Barbara the next day, Mom says, "We have time if you want to stop and see the Mission."

"No," I say. "I don't want to go." To see the Mission would mean my wish came true. I want to erase the wish. I want to erase myself.

"It's all you've been talking about." Mom stops and looks at me closely. "What's wrong?" She draws me to her and I can't hold it inside any longer.

I confess. Frankie and I upset Dad. My wish got granted. It's all my fault.

Mom listens, then quietly tells me it's impossible my fighting with Frankie or my wish to see the Mission made Dad die. "There was something wrong with his heart for a long time. The doctors told me months ago he only had a little while left." She brushes the hair from my face. "By believing your wish caused him to die, I think you're trying to believe you could have changed what happened. You want to think you could have saved him."

She is right.

My head rests against her chest and I can hear her heart beating. I cry a good long time, and then Mom dries my tears and we drive to the Mission. When we round the corner, the apricot-colored bell towers come into view and I let out a little gasp, it is so beautiful. Mom parks the car and we walk together up to the fountain in front of the Mission. I reach out and touch the water in the fountain with my fingers and make the sign of the cross, just like when I enter Church. We see the chapel and the living quarters and the aqueduct and it all looks like the model my father helped me make. Everything I see reminds me of him.

Monday, I am back in school and there is something very comforting about seeing Mrs. Webb, about having her smile at me and seeing that gap between her front teeth.

"I have a presentation to make," Mrs. Webb says, and calls me to the front of the room where she puts her arm around my shoulders. "We all know how much it's meant to you to study the Missions, and so the school has bought a book." She holds up a thick hardbound copy of The California Missions. On the cover is a photograph of adobe arches, just like the ones my father helped me cut out of Styrofoam.

Mrs. Webb opens up to the first page and reads her own handwritten words. "This book is dedicated to the memory of Louie Sacconaghi, the father of Jeannie Sacconaghi. The Burton School Library, March 7, 1965."

I can't help it. Even though I am up there in front of everybody, I cry.

My father and I are linked together by the Mission in Santa Barbara. My wish to go there really had been my wish to claim the place where he was born as my own. By making it belong to me, I felt I belonged to him. My teacher's words etched in ink are proof that I have succeeded.

"Louie Sacconaghi, the father of Jeannie..."

8

Every morning, Dad used to peek through the heavy blue bedroom drapes to check the weather, then bend down and wake Mom with a kiss. Now he is gone and Mom gets a radio alarm clock and Dave McElhattan on KCBS wakes her up every morning. He calls Ranger Rick up on Mount Diablo. "What's the weather look like up there today?"

"Looks like rain,"says Ranger Rick. Dave and Ranger Rick make her focus on the view from Mount Diablo instead of the view from her bedroom window.

We are not the only family that death visits. Another man who works at my father's company loses his wife to cancer. The man has two children close in age to Frankie and me, so it is logical for our two families to get together for dinner to console each other. But grief is not a logical thing.

"Betty," the grieving man says to my mom, his third drink sloshing in his glass. "You can't keep this bottled up inside. You need to let it out."

Mom grits her teeth and examines the flower arrangement on the coffee table. She was raised in Ohio where people don't tell each other what to do or how to feel. I come over and sit on her knee. "I want to go home," I whisper in her ear.

The grieving man gestures me aside. "Go watch television with my kids."

Frankie and the grieving man's kids are watching an old black and white movie about a giant one-eyed alien named Cronos who is taking over the Earth. When he kills several people with his laser beam eye, I run back to Mom.

She has a heavy glass tumbler in her hand, a drink the grieving man has fixed for her. The next day she will tell me he gave her something called a Mickey Finn. I try to squeeze onto her lap, but her arms are crossed. She is a fortress, keeping everyone at bay. "I want to go home." I don't bother to whisper this time.

"Your mother needs to talk," says the grieving man, tears in his eyes. I know my mother hasn't said a word. *He* is the one who needs to talk, but I don't think my mom needs to hear anything he has to say. He reaches out and takes the tumbler from Mom's hand, walking back to the bar to refill it. "Go back with the other kids," he says to me.

"They're watching a scary movie. Please, Mom. I want to go."

Mom looks at me, her eyes ever-so-slightly crossed and she rubs my back for a moment. "We'll go after dinner."

I am not hungry. I go back to the television room. I don't want to watch Cronos as he hypnotizes the main characters, causing them to walk around like Zombies, doing whatever Cronos wants them to.

When the clock chimes nine, a slightly burnt casserole is removed from the oven. I eat only slices of white bread with butter and Mom doesn't tell me I have to eat anything else. Her eyes have a spacey look to them, like the humans that Cronos has taken control of. When everyone is finally done eating, I plead, "Can we go home now?"

"I suppose," Mom says faintly.

The night air is cold and I can see the stars above as the grieving man walks us to the driveway. "Do you have to leave so early?" He glares at me, then tries to kiss Mom, more than a peck on the cheek, but she waves him away as if he is a fly and gets shakily into the car.

It is only a five minute drive to La Cañada Road. Mom lurches our white Ford station wagon out into the street and shifts into drive. I look through the back window of the car and watch the grieving man become smaller and smaller behind us.

No one says a word as we drive through the darkness toward home. Mom's eyes are riveted on the white line that runs down the middle of St. Mary's Road, keeping the car centered on it. "Mom," says Frankie. "Aren't you supposed to stay on the right side of the line?"

"I am."

Frankie and I share a look. Something is very wrong. Mom turns the station wagon onto our dirt road, the car bouncing hard in the ruts.

"Mom," I say. "You're driving too fast!"

"When you're old enough to drive," she slurs, "then you can tell me how to drive."

Our station wagon veers around the corner by Perrelli's house, then weaves toward the right and the Wilson's mailbox flies up over the hood. "Mom!" Frankie and I shriek in unison. "You hit their mailbox!"

"What mailbox?"

She gets the Stithem's mailbox next, and then the Teft's before we finally pull into our driveway, home at last. Mom refuses to believe she hit anything. Her hand shakes as she tries to get the key into the door of our house.

"You want me to do that?" Frankie asks.

She sneers at him. "I know how to unlock a door young man." Inside, she plops down on the tall maple chair next to the phone in the family room, then notices us standing warily in the corner. "Go to bed," she snaps.

Frankie and I are only too happy to oblige. I put on my light blue flannel pajamas and crawl between the sheets, my bedroom door open, a comforting shaft of light coming from the hallway. And then I hear a sound I have never heard before. My mother is crying.

I climb out of bed and pad down the hallway to the family room and peer inside. There is my mother slumped in the tall chair, sobbing, trying to dial our rotary phone. "Mom?" She doesn't answer me, and I move in closer, slowly, as if I am approaching an animal that has been hit by a car. "Mom?"

She turns, her eyes red, full of tears. I know I should be afraid. We are not supposed to see her like this, we are supposed to fall apart if she cries. But I am not afraid. My hand moves to her back, to rub it gently, the way she rubbed mine just hours before.

"Go to bed honey," she says, her voice broken by sobs.

I don't move. "Who're you calling?"

"Lue... Margaret... someone..."

"Let me dial."

"No," she sobs. "Just go back to bed. Please."

I know she really wants me to go, that she doesn't want me to see her like this, but I am not going to leave her alone. I put my arms around her, and her head falls upon my shoulder and she cries. I don't know how long we stand like that, her on the tall maple chair bent into my nine-year-old shoulder, me standing upright, rubbing her back, as if our roles are reversed.

Her husband is dead and she can no longer hold in her grief. It is not something people in Ohio do, burden others with their problems. But I am not just anyone. I am her daughter. I have never felt my role so strongly.

I have been her daughter from the day I was three months old and a social worker placed me in her arms, but on this night, I am reborn. I feel it. I *am* my mother's daughter. I know that no one else can love her any more than I do at this moment, not even a daughter who has come out of her body.

It is the greatest gift my mother has ever given me, letting me hold her, letting me comfort her, letting me see her at her most vulnerable. I know people from Ohio do that only with members of their own family.

9

The leaders of our Girl Scout troop take us on an outing to the tiny park in the heart of Lafayette. A man from the town council meets us there to talk to us about the history of our town. "Today I'm going to talk about the first Americans to live in this valley," he says. "It begins with this grindstone." He rests his hand upon the only monument in the park, a round stone embedded in pebbled cement.

Covering maybe fifty square yards, Lafayette's has the smallest registered park in the United States. There isn't any room to run or play, only enough space for us to hover around him beside this stone.

"There were few landed gentry in early California," our speaker continues. "Instead, our pioneering forefathers were risk takers and gamblers. Lafayette was founded by one of the former, a man named Elam Brown who crossed the same trail as the Donner Party, and made it over the pass a mere two weeks ahead of that ill-fated group."

"Boring," Debbie whispers over my shoulder.

"Shh," I say. "I want to hear this."

"Touch it," the man from the town council encourages us, running his hand across the top of the stone. "This is what history feels like." In awe, my hand follows his across the rough surface.

Other girls are giggling, no longer paying attention, but I am riveted on the man from the town council. He is talking about history, about descendants who came before us, a matter of great seriousness to me. "Our earliest connection with our ancestors is not found in books," he says, after the leaders have shushed the girls. "It doesn't come from words or pictures. It comes from stone, from relics of stone, be they arrowheads or blocks of a pyramid or grinding wheels."

I am in his church now. I understand what he means, my hand caressing the rough stone. "When we can place our hand and touch where our ancestors touched," he says, "we can literally feel their world. It is our only way of truly touching them."

I am his entire congregation. My arms circle the stone, embracing Elam Brown and all our Lafayette ancestors.

"Are we having a snack?" someone asks.

"Hostess cupcakes," Debbie says. "My mom brought Hostess cupcakes. And Welches grape juice."

"Shh!" our leader says. "Listen to what he's saying. This is a requirement for your badge."

"But I'm hungry."

"You won't get your badge."

I barely hear any of this. I am in Lafayette, in 1846. The past fills me up in a way that cupcakes and grape juice cannot.

"This one seemed interested," the man says, nodding in my direction as we eat our snack on the tiny patch of grass.

"I'm going to be a historian," I say. I sit with my back against the grindstone, the touchstone for my future.

A week later, Debbie and I ride our bikes downtown to the Lafayette Toy Store, right across the street from the park. We each have a dime to buy a candy bar at the market, and come into the toy store only to see the new Beatles wigs that have just come out. Debbie giggles, placing a moppish brunette wig on each of our heads. She strains, staring at the store window, trying to see her reflection in the glass. "I love John Lennon," she declares.

I look past our reflection to the grinding wheel in the park and wonder what Elam Brown would think of the Beatles wig on my head. I wonder what he would think of all the streets and the cars and the thousands of people who now live in the town he founded a hundred years ago. What would he think about the Ed Sullivan Show and jet airplanes and men walking in space? If he were standing beside me, looking out the same window I am, would he open the door and walk outside, or would he run and hide under the counter?

"Which Beatle do you want to marry?" Debbie asks.

I struggle for a moment to remember who the Beatles even are. I look at Debbie blankly and blurt out, "Elam."

"Elam?" She is looking at me like I'm crazy.

"He's one of the Rolling Stones," I say quickly. It works. She doesn't know the names of all the Rolling Stones. I look out at the grinding wheel and smile.

10

Jan and I lean against the rail of the thick-beamed bridge which spans La Cañada Creek, throwing buckeyes stripped of their hides into the shallow water below. "Watch this one," Jan says, hurling one far past my last effort, making a splash downstream.

We meet the summer I am eleven and dress identically in blue jeans and t-shirts and black high-top sneakers. We are one.

"Where are you going?" Mom asks.

"Jan's."

After a while, Mom stops asking. She knows where to find me.

We do a hundred cannonballs off Jan's diving board and play make-believe games based on television shows, pretending to be characters from *McHale's Navy* and *Flipper*. Her dog, Sloopy, barks at us from the edge of the pool and we sing to him, "Hang on Sloopy, Sloopy hang on!"

We both love animals. Between us we have dogs and cats and hamsters and rats and pigeons and rabbits and a baby buzzard. At least once a week we ride our three-speed bikes to the pet store in downtown Lafayette and walk through the maze of aquariums and cages.

One day Jan is at the pet store and thinks she sees me in the next aisle. She sneaks up and pokes the girl from behind, laughing, but when the girl turns around, Jan realizes it is not me, but another girl with the same color hair, the same color eyes, wearing jeans and high-top sneakers. "You look just like my best friend," says Jan.

This is how lifelong relationships can begin.

"What's your name?" Jan asks.

"Linda," says the girl.

When Jan invites her over to play, I am jealous. Jan is *my* best friend. I don't want to be replaced by some clone of myself. But then we swim in the pool. "Let's play Flipper," says Jan. "You be Sandy and I'll be Bud."

"Okay," I say. "Who do you want to be?" I ask the new girl who looks like me.

"I'll be Flipper."

I grin. "Cool." She makes great dolphin noises and can hold her breath under water for over a minute. Instantly, we are a threesome.

Linda invites us to her house to play and we meet her mom who looks like a movie star and her dad who looks like John Wayne and her two brothers. But first, she introduces us to the most important person in her house. "This is Cindy," says Linda, her arm draped around a black Labrador Retriever. Cindy wags her thick tail as we pat her gray muzzle.

We get into our swimsuits and jump into Linda's Doughboy pool. Cindy follows us and flops down on the wooden deck and goes to sleep while the three of us discover that if we all swim hard in the same direction, we can make a whirlpool that will carry us along. Swim, swim, swim, float, laugh hysterically. Swim, swim, float, laugh, over and over.

Only hunger intrudes on the game. Linda's mother brings us tunafish sandwiches and we dry off and eat. Linda saves her last bite. "Here Cindy," she says, holding out the sandwich.

Cindy doesn't respond.

"Wake up girl," she laughs, putting the tunafish sandwich right under her dog's nose.

The dog does not move. Jan and I glance at each other as Linda bends down. "Cindy?" She gently rocks the big black dog and blood rushes from the dog's nose. "Cindy!"

I run and get her parents. Everyone in the family hurries out to where Linda is bent over, hugging her dog, sobbing, "Come on girl, wake up!"

Cindy is dead. Linda can barely breathe as her father wraps the old Labrador in a blanket and places her in the back of his International Scout. The three of us stand at the edge of the driveway and watch as the Scout disappears down the hill.

"I know how you feel," I say to Linda. "My dad died last year."

Linda nods, her eyes swollen and red. The three of us sit on the railing of her redwood deck overlooking the Diablo Valley and Linda tells us stories about her dog.

I only knew Cindy for two hours before she died, but she will be a part of us, always. She is some of the glue that holds the three of us together. We are bound by many things, things we have in common and things still to come. But we begin with the loss of an old black dog and a long vigil on a sunny afternoon.

Cindy made the three of us into a family.

11

After Dad dies, Grandpa moves to Whittier to live with my Aunt Rena, his sole surviving child. As he carefully loads his potted orchids into the moving van, I secretly hope he'll give me one to take care of, but he doesn't. Instead he ruffles my hair and climbs into the front seat of the truck next to the driver. And he is gone.

Out in the empty hothouse, I sit upon the rough-hewn boards of the planter shelf, my knees tucked under my chin. The air is thick with scents of Grandpa's fertilizer and earth and Old World sweat. I sit for a long time, thinking.

"Can I have a horse?" I ask that night at dinner.

"We don't have enough room for a horse," Mom replies.

"We could turn Grandpa's hothouse into a barn."

"No horse."

"Well how about an elephant then?" Mom looks up and smiles. When Dad was alive, I incessantly begged for a dog or a cat, but Dad wasn't fond of pets and would always say, "I only like elephants, but we don't have enough room for an elephant so..."

After his death, Mom tries to compensate for the empty space in our home by getting us black kittens we name Scrooge and Ringo. The cats are followed by sixty-four rats (there were only two in the beginning), a duck named Ralph, a German Shepherd named Brandy, an Irish Setter named Christy, and after a year of convincing her, a horse named Stonewall Jackson.

He is a tall, chunky chestnut with a white blaze. The hothouse is turned into a barn to store his hay and tack, and we fence the bottom corner of our third acre lot. Where Grandpa once cultivated cucumbers and corn and fruit trees full of apricots and figs, I now cultivate my dream of owning a horse.

The afternoon Stoney arrives in our driveway, stomping his feet impatiently in the back of a horse trailer, I don't wait a minute. I put on his bridle and lead him to the edge of Grandpa's raised vegetable beds, boost myself up onto his bare back, and we are off. I guide him across the wooden bridge spanning La Cañada creek and into a walnut orchard, sitting dreamily, sixteen hands above the ground.

Suddenly, Stoney takes hold of the bit in his mouth and bolts across the orchard. It doesn't take a very large branch to remove me from his bare back, just some low slender twigs, and I am sitting on the ground, watching Stoney's chestnut rump disappear in a cloud of dust, the bridle reins flapping wildly at his sides. I have been a horse owner for less than half an hour and I've already lost my horse.

He turns up outside Jan's corral, nose to nose with her horse Cheetah and on my second day as a horse owner, things get better. Jan and I saddle-up, our games of make-believe now extending far out into the rolling hills. "There are these bank robbers hiding out in the creek," I say. "They kidnap you and Cheetah, and we rescue you."

"Okay," says Jan, tapping her horse lightly with her heels. I make Stoney wait a minute or two, until things are looking really grim, and only then do we race off to rescue the victims.

My horse never throws me again and together he and I save Jan and Cheetah from every possible fate. Still, owning a horse doesn't quite match my fantasy. My imagination is too influenced by my Saturday morning idol, "Fury", a black stallion who won't let anyone else on his back except his young master, a horse who is loyal, a best friend.

Stoney's grudging commitment to me is coerced daily by alfalfa and oats. He is a good horse, probably the perfect horse for me. His bad habits are few and he is a predictable sort of guy, slow on the way out, fast on the way home. But he isn't Fury. He isn't even close.

One stormy winter afternoon, long after Stoney left me in the dust of the walnut orchard, I sit in the hothouse listening to the rain falling upon the fiberglass roof. Grandpa's Old World sweat has been replaced by the pungent odor of hay and grain, and I lean back against a four-by-four post, pull a long strand of alfalfa from a bale, and chew on it, thinking. My horse has taught me something about my grandfather.

Stoney is as unlike Fury as Grandpa is unlike Gus the Fireman.

Grandpa dies the summer of 1969, just before Woodstock and Chappaquidick and Neil and Buzz landing on the moon. He is in northern Italy when it happens, visiting Lonate Pozzolo, the little town where he was born. As my grandfather reads a letter informing him of the death of a friend, he has a heart attack and dies.

The last time I saw him was at the Oakland Airport. He was flying to Italy on a chartered plane and Mom and I met him for lunch in between his flight in from Los Angeles and his flight out to Milan. In the airport cafeteria there were dozens of men who looked exactly like Giuseppe Sacconaghi, old stocky men wearing felt hats and worn coats with leather patches on the elbows.

Grandpa didn't say much as I chattered away during lunch, telling him about the chestnut horse we had living in his vegetable garden. Later, when I gave him a hug goodbye at the gate, his coat smelled exactly like the hothouse did the day he left us, and I held on to him for a moment, just to breathe in that memory, never thinking it would be the last time I touched him.

A month later, I received something in the mail I never received before: a postcard from my grandfather all the way from Italy. His handwriting was uneven and difficult to decipher mainly because, except for my name and address, the entire card was written in Italian. But I understood what the card said even if I couldn't read his words.

On the postcard was a picture of a chestnut horse with a white blaze. My grandfather sent me something he knew I would love. That was as good as him telling me he loved me himself.

12

The helicopter blades begin slowly at first, slicing a big sweeping arc above our heads. Whoosh! Whoosh! Mom huddles her face next to mine at the window and peers upward.

It is my twelfth birthday and this adventure is Mom's idea. We are flying in a large commuter helicopter all the way from Lafayette to the San Francisco Airport. When she reveals her surprise outing, I shrug. "Okay."

"Okay?" says Mom . "I thought you'd be jumping up and down."

"Oh." I give a little jump and grin.

"Why, I would have given anything to travel when I was your age."

I stop smiling and brace for *the* speech.

"We didn't have the things you kids have. There was the Depression. No one had money to travel." I sigh. I know all about the Depression. Once a month, Mom cooks what she calls the Depression dinner: creamed chipped beef on toast. "We had to eat this almost every night when I was your age."

The Depression dinners are supposed to teach Frankie and me about sacrifice, about how scary it can be when there isn't much money and one's very survival is in question. The problem is, I love her chipped beef. "This is great!" I say, holding out my plate for more.

Mom grimaces. "Imagine if you had to eat it every night."

"Can we?"

When I lose ten Bic pens during my first semester of middle school, Mom says, "My father gave me a fountain pen when I graduated from the sixth grade, and that one pen saw me all the way through high school."

"Oh." She scans my face to see if I really do understand. I nod earnestly and wait thirty seconds before asking, "So can I have a dollar to ride my bike downtown and get some more pens?"

She shakes her head sadly, reaching for the worn leather billfold she has had for as long as I can remember. She does not say a word as she hands me the dollar, but I know she believes I will never understand what it means to do without.

The noise from the helicopter blades is deafening. I glance around at the twenty other people on board, all businessmen in dark suits with white shirts and thin ties. None of them seems very excited. "Here we go!" Mom gasps with delight, as if she is the one who is twelve. I know I am about to do something my mother never got to do at my age: soar straight up into the air in a helicopter. Mom is trying to give me everything she never got as a child.

On the last Thursday of the nineteenth century, Mom's parents were married in Ohio, and Effie Brumbaugh moved five miles down the road from the house where she was born in Brookville to Stanley Wenger's farm. Over the next twenty-one years, she gave birth to seven children. Her first son died in infancy. Her second, Arden, born the year the Wright brothers flew at Kittyhawk, died after being struck in the head with a baseball when he was fourteen. He was survived by his sisters, Ruth, Bernice, Marty, and Dorothy. My mom, Betty Lou, wasn't born until four years later.

She was eight-years-old when the Depression hit. Her father, a minister, got a job at the local pharmacy to keep food on the table. There wasn't much money, certainly not enough for a helicopter ride.

Mom would climb to the top of Brookville's water tower, sitting on the edge of the catwalk, fifty feet above the ground, and gaze off into the distance, dreaming of adventures beyond Brookville's borders. She graduated from business college in 1941 and became a secretary for an Army colonel. When an opportunity arose for her to transfer to a base in California, she jumped at the chance.

Her mother cried. "We'll never see you again."

"I'll come home every five years," Mom promised, and she kept her word, visiting Brookville after V-J Day to introduce her new husband, Captain Louie Sacconaghi, to her family. Before Mom returned again, however, her mother had a heart attack and died in the house five miles down the road from where she was born.

I never met my Grandma Wenger. There is a picture of her on Mom's dresser. Her gray hair pulled back, she is wearing wire-rimmed glasses and the hint of a smile. She looks like the kind of grandmother who would bake great cookies. I imagine her to be like my four aunts.

The Wenger sisters can talk a blue streak, able to maintain five individual conversations at the same time. I love to hear them laughing with my mother, to hear their big family noise. I adore them, and they love me, I can tell. Whenever we visit Ohio, they tell me stories about when I was little, making me know I am part of the family.

"Jeannie, you've gotten so tall." Aunt Marty's voice sounds just like Mom's. "Why I can remember when you were six, and you tried to catch lightning bugs in our backyard, and they were up here," she says, holding her hand to her eye level, "Just beyond your reach."

"You loaded that wagon in my garage with all my old pop bottles and pulled them down to the corner store," says Aunt Bernice, "and then gave me the fifty-seven cents you got. I'll never forget that."

"I'll never forget the first time I saw you," says Aunt Ruth. "You were only two."

"You had the biggest blue eyes I'd ever seen." Aunt Dorothy smiles.

"You were glad to get off the plane," says Aunt Bernice. "Remember?"

"It hurt your ears," says Marty. "You told me so and you were only two."

"Your mother said you didn't like looking out the windows of the plane. You cried and cried."

The helicopter lifts off and an eerie sensation fills my stomach, as if I am falling upward. Mom and I are suddenly a hundred feet in the air. I pull back from the window and tighten my seatbelt.

I pick up the big white envelope on the kitchen counter and look at it curiously. "What's this?"

"A family tree," says Mom. "A Wenger cousin put it together."

A family tree! The blank piece of manila paper flashes through my mind, Mrs. Stadleman's assignment all those years ago. "Can I see it?"

There is a slight hesitation before Mom says, "Sure."

Inside are several pages stapled together listing family members all the way back to the 1700's. I flip through it until I reach the section that has all the information about the five Wenger sisters. There are my four aunts, all my cousins. And there is Mom, and Frankie and me! A family tree, a family I belong to. Except...

I look closely at the page. Underneath my name is a word in parentheses.

(Adopted)

None of my cousins have any words written under their names. I stare at the word. I still tell kids at my school that being adopted means I am special. But seeing the word like that doesn't make me feel special, it makes me feel different, as if my membership in the family requires an explanation, a disclaimer.

"Made me angry," Mom says, even though I haven't said anything.

"Really?"

Jean Anne Sacconaghi   4-12-55
(Adopted)

"Belonging to a family has nothing to do with words," Mom says. "It's about sharing life together."

I know she's not lying. She's not saying this to try to make me feel better. She is telling me the truth. I *am* a part of her family. She puts the stapled pages back in the envelope and sticks it in the bottom of a drawer in her desk.

The helicopter is rising higher in the air now, moving away from the heliport in Lafayette. "Look at the cars on the freeway," says Mom, pointing. "Look how small they are, like toys!"

We are a thousand feet in the air, two thousand, rising higher and higher, and I open my eyes to find out she's right, everything does look like toys. I add my voice to Mom's. "Hey look! There's the Orinda Theater! There's the tunnel! The Bay Bridge!"

"See the Golden Gate!"

"Wow!"

We are travelers, my mother and me. Together, we are doing something she has always dreamed of doing, high in the sky, having an adventure. We are making memories, memories that show we belong to each other. They are more important than any words on a page.

13

The last day I see my Grandpa Wenger, I become a griot.

I am fourteen and Grandpa is over ninety and living in a nursing home in Ohio. The afternoon we're to visit him, Mom hands me a pair of nylons, along with a skirt and nice shoes.

I have never worn nylons in my life and stand in my cutoffs and sneakers looking at them with disdain. "Why do I have to wear these? He won't care how I look."

"Please," Mom says in her nice suit. "I care."

I glance at her and suddenly understand: this is the last time she will see her father. I don't say anything more about having to wear the nice clothes or the nylons. She shows me how to inch my hands all the way down to the toe of the stockings and then slide them on. I pull too hard and make a huge run. Mom has an extra pair, and I manage to get them on without destroying them. They feel tight and constricting. "Yuck," I say under my breath and Mom pretends she hasn't heard.

We walk down the shiny waxed hallway of the nursing home toward my grandfather's room. I follow my mother's feet in front of me, wrinkling my nose at the scent of Mr. Clean and bedpans that hangs in the air, and almost run smack into Mom when she stops abruptly in the doorway of her father's room.

It takes her a moment to adjust to the sight. There is her father, sunken back against the sheets, much smaller than the last time we saw him. His skin seems transparent, his blue veins like a road map upon his arms.

Mom smooths her skirt and steps inside. His eyes follow her as she approaches and bends down, smiling. "Hi Dad," she says, kissing his cheek.

He stares up at her. "Who are you?"

Mom's face pales as she explains she is his daughter. She is Betty.

Stanley Wenger studies her, confused. "Betty? I don't know any Betty."

Mom sits down on the edge of the bed and gently picks up her father's hand. I stand, transfixed, for what seems like an hour, as Mom talks softly, stroking his hand until her father falls asleep. Only then does she stand up to leave. At the door, she pauses and looks back, but I don't. How would I feel if Mom didn't know *me*? I never look back at my grandfather. Not once.

After dinner at Aunt Ruth's, Mom sits in a chair in the backyard, smoking a cigarette, staring off into space. I want to go out and sit with her, but Aunt Ruth asks me to help her wash the dishes. "Did I ever tell you about your great grandfather Wenger?" she asks.

"No."

"He died half a century ago, and I was thinking today about something Dad taught me that his father taught him." Aunt Ruth clears her throat and recites, "Would you be so kind and condescending and gratify me so much as to extricate my quadruped from the vehicle, stabulate and donate him with the proper quantities of nutritious elements, and when the rural of the morn has illuminated, I will present you with a handsome reward."

I laugh. "What's it mean?"

"That's how he'd instruct a tavern owner to unhitch his horse and stable it for the night, with the promise he'd reimburse him in the morning."

"It sounds like a foreign language."

Aunt Ruth nods. "It's strange how much has changed in such a short time." She hands me a plate to dry. "Those words are the only way I know my grandfather. They are my window to his world."

I look past my aunt, through the steam-fogged kitchen window, to where my mother sits on the patio. "How's that go again?"

"Would you be so kind . . ."

I spend the evening memorizing it and later, when I kiss Mom goodnight, I proudly recite the nineteenth-century words. "Aunt Ruth said Grandpa taught her that," I say. "It was something his father taught him."

For the first time all day, my mother smiles.

At the end of his book <u>Roots</u>, Alex Haley talks about the oral historians of Central Africa, individuals who recite by memory entire family histories. These people are called *griots*.

I become a griot the summer I am fourteen by committing to memory an old saying passed down from my mother's grandfather. These words link me not only to her, but to her father, and his father before him. It is my gift to my mother on the day her father no longer remembers who she is.

I will remember him and all who came before.

14

A redwood branch scratches my face as I push through the trees behind our house. "He went down there," I point, and the three sheriff deputies follow my hand. I am telling them how to find Frankie.

This is not the first time.

I glance back at Mom on the patio with another deputy, the Camel she holds between her fingers shaking, even though her voice is calm. My mother is not leading the deputies toward the creek. I am. "Down there," I point.

Two of the deputies begin to run. They have seen something. Branches crack beneath their feet. "Stop!" they shout in unison.

I can see Frankie now, in flight, a sixteen-year-old blur of white t-shirt and black Chinos, disappearing over the edge of the creek bank. The remaining deputy puts his hand on my arm. "Wait here. This might be dangerous." I don't argue. In the past months there have been threats. Fists. Screamed obscenities. Stolen cars and money. And voices. Frankie is hearing voices we cannot hear.

Footfalls splash across the creek. "Stop! Stop!" the deputies yell at Frankie, like hounds, baying.

The deputy who has remained behind pats my shoulder gently. "You're a good kid," he says.

Everyone tells me I'm a good kid. I'm not sure they're right. I am helping the police catch my brother. I'm not sure what that makes me. I watch from the kitchen window as the deputies put him in the back of a patrol car. Mom looks so small standing there on the driveway, her face white, like the smoke from yet another Camel drifting skyward.

That night, as I sleep in my bedroom, a sound invades my slumber, a tapping. I roll over and open my eyes, and there is Frankie, tapping on my window pane, a flashlight grotesquely illuminating his face. He has escaped from the county mental health facility. Again.

I fling myself from the bed, screaming. Mom calls the sheriff and does not open the back door to let Frankie in. He paces back and forth like a tiger in a cage, yelling obscenities at us from the patio, until the siren of a patrol car causes him to run from our yard. It begins all over again, the chase, the shouts in the dark.

"We can only keep him for seventy-two hours," the county psychiatrist informs her. "Unless you want to file criminal charges. But I'll warn you, imprisoning him will expose him to horrible things and horrible people."

Mom takes Frankie to another doctor, then another. The diagnosis is always the same: paranoid schizophrenia. He is given medication which he holds under his tongue and does not swallow, later spitting the pills into the sink, the toilet, anywhere.

Mom's hair goes from brunette to gray.

My friends ask why my brother has the word "NATAS" written on his forehead in bold black laundry marker ink. I explain that he is actually writing "SATAN." It's only backwards because he writes it while looking in the mirror.

"How could this happen?" my mother asks.

"We don't know what causes schizophrenia," one doctor tells her.

A social worker with thinning strands of hair pasted from one side of his head to the other says, "It is something in his upbringing, something you have done." He says this as I sit beside my mother in a nicely upholstered chair in his office.

I leap to my feet. "If that's true, how come I'm okay!" Bastard. I am only fifteen, but the word is on the tip of my tongue. He looks at me sadly, and shrugs at my mother, as if to indicate that in my case, too, it is only a matter of time. I stare him down, defiant, then blink, wondering, who would lead the police to their own brother?

Frankie breaks out of the county mental facility again, this time with another patient, and the two of them hitch a ride to La Cañada Road. It is

minutes, he changes all the rules. He gives me permission to do something I have wanted to do since the third grade. He tells me I can search.

So I begin. I have no idea what to do. There are no books in the library that can advise me how to go about finding someone whose name I don't even know. But when I am home for Christmas, I open the family safe and take the old file folder Mom handed me long ago.

I do not ask her or tell her that I am taking it. I am a burglar in my mother's house, but I rationalize my theft. If my searching could cause her pain, there is no need for her to know what I am doing unless I find someone. I am willing to steal the file, but not to break my mother's heart. I tell myself I can live with this subterfuge.

This will cost me.

I study every piece of paper in the file. Each one contains clues. I know most of them by heart. *Last name, Porter. Her name, probably. A woman, five foot four, with blue eyes and light brown hair. A secretary, born in Portland, Oregon, on August 10, 1934.* I have no idea what to do with any of this information.

For a journalism class, I write an essay about my desire to search and when the professor, John Riley, passes the paper back to me, he asks me how it's going.

"Well, I sort of haven't done anything yet."

"Why not?"

"I don't know how to start."

He asks to borrow my file. I relinquish it hesitantly. What if parts of it become lost? But the following week, John Riley hands the file safely back to me with a typed note attached. "What's this?" I ask.

"The address and phone number of the doctor who delivered you."

"How'd you get it?"

"His name's on your birth certificate. I just looked him up."

"Oh."

John Riley can tell by the confused look on my face that he's dealing with someone a couple sandwiches shy of a picnic. "Think. Doctors keep records. If he has records of your birth, he might have your birth mother's name."

Lightbulbs click on in my head. I race home and call the doctor who is very nice and understanding. If he had the information I am asking for, he would give it to me, but he was merely a resident at the hospital in 1955 and has no record of my birth nor any recollection of my delivery almost three decades ago. Despite the fact that I have reached my first dead end, it is exciting to talk to the doctor whose hands were the first human touch I ever received.

Buoyed, I ask John Riley after class the following week, "What else can I do?"

A former investigative reporter for *Life* magazine, he has a lot of ideas. I know when and where my birth mother was born and the name she gave me. He suggests I order microfilm copies of Portland, Oregon newspapers for the late summer and fall of 1934 to look for birth announcements of a baby girl born on August 10th with the last name of Porter.

To John Riley's surprise and my dismay, there isn't one. I am able to find five baby girls born on that date, but not one of them is named Porter. One, however, is named Anne. "Maybe that's her," says John Riley. "Your whole given name at birth might be a clue. Cecilia *Anne* Porter. She might well have given you one of her names by naming you that."

I write down the information about the baby girl named Anne, along with the other four, just in case, and put them in the file folder that contains everything else I know. Next, I write to the agency that handled my adoption. Even though I already have an information sheet the agency gave my parents in 1955, I ask for my file. A social worker writes me back, explaining that she cannot give me any identifying information, but she tells me something new, something which explains why I wasn't able to find a baby girl named Porter in the Portland newspapers.

Your (birth mother) was described as an attractive, healthy, intelligent young woman... She, too, was adopted.

My strongest clues instantly become meaningless. My birth mother is an adoptee, just like me. There will be no record of her birth anywhere. But while the social worker discourages me with this piece of news, she inspires me with a paragraph later on.

You were relinquished when you were 3 days old. We received a letter from your mother 5 years later; she wanted to be sure you had been placed with a Catholic family. She also said she was married and had four children. We have heard nothing further from her.

I reread this paragraph over and over. My birth mother *wrote* to them. She wanted to know if I was all right. To me, this means she wouldn't mind being found. My birth mother stamps my search passport with a letter she wrote a quarter century ago.

And heart stopping: I have four brothers and sisters. I never thought of having other siblings besides Frank. The very notion overwhelms me. "Marsha, Marsha, Marsha." I am a member of the Brady Bunch. Four brothers and sisters! I will not rest until I find them.

Not everyone is nice to me when I ask for information. I write to the hospital where I was born, requesting medical records for myself and my birth mother, and when I don't hear from the hospital, I decide to go there in person. I am nervous. Even though all I am doing is asking for information about myself, somehow I feel I have no right to ask for anything. I take a deep breath outside the records office before stepping inside and manage to explain to a young receptionist that I had requested some records by mail and just happened to be in the area and thought I'd stop by and pick them up.

The receptionist says, "Your name rings a bell," and she turns to a shelf, then back to me with two file folders in her hand. "These are the records you requested," she says, placing the files, one on top of the other, on her desk right in front of me. "Just a moment. There's something I need to check with my supervisor."

She steps away from desk and begins speaking to a woman a few steps away, her back to me. My eyes are riveted on the two files. The top one has the name 'Cecilia Anne Porter' on the tab. That means the one directly beneath it has my birth mother's name. The identity of my birth mother is right there in front of me.

Seconds tick by while I sit motionless in the chair. A voice inside my head is screaming for me to grab the folders and run. But I can envision police chasing me through the halls of the hospital, like my brother through the creek bed, grabbing me before I get very far, leading me away in handcuffs, the mug shot of me from the front and the side, the phone being held out for me in jail to make my one phone call, and me saying what? "Hi Mom. Gosh, you won't believe what I've been up to today..."

A minute elapses. If I only had the presence of mind to simply stand up and slide the files apart, I might have gotten my birth mother's name, but a shadow falls across the files on the desk and I look up and meet the supervisor. The look in her eyes makes me feel like crawling under a rock.

"We have not sent your records because you are adopted." She clutches the files tightly to her chest. "You have no right to any of this information."

I flush bright red. The young receptionist is peering at me, as if I have been caught passing bad checks. My voice shakes as I try to remember what John Riley told me about the new law concerning medical records. "I understood that by law, uh, you know, AB 610 or something, that I have a right, uh, to medical records, you know, concerning me." That's telling her Jean!

"These records are sealed," the supervisor says sharply. A small group of workers now circles the young receptionist, whispering. They are glancing at me, the sideshow, today's entertainment for filing clerks.

I stand, wishing I had taken the records and run, and wishing my voice wasn't shaking. "I'm just looking for my medical background."

"We will mail you a copy of what's in your file only after we have whited out every piece of identifying information." Her voice is full of accusations.

Tears sting my eyes as she opens the door, showing me the way out. No police are waiting for me at the main entrance, and I slink toward the parking lot, the anger building inside me with every step. I'm just trying to find out about where I came from. Is that a crime? No one else's records need to be whited out. Does seeking my roots mean I deserve to be humiliated?

The hospital supervisor becomes one of my teachers. Her lesson is prejudice. It was there, clearly, in her eyes as she looked at me: she viewed me as inferior. I feel her lurking behind me as my every attempt to find my birth family fails. She is there at the County Recorders office when I look up my birth record.

There is no record on file for Jean Anne Sacconaghi. According to the county where I was born, I do not exist. But there *is* a record for Cecilia Anne Porter. When I see this, my heart leaps. Is my original birth certificate on file?

My hands shake as I submit a request for the roll of microfilm. The clerk behind the counter gives me a second look and I try hard not to grab the microfilm from her hands in my rush to a projector. I am going to see my birth mother's name! It is right here in this office and these nice people are going to let me see it, just like that. I spin the microfilm reel, faster and faster, until I get to April and then I slow the projector to a snails pace. When my birth certificate rolls into view I stop and stare.

Except for the name Cecilia Anne Porter and the date, April 12, everything else has been whited out. I can hear the hospital records supervisor cackling in my mind. "You have no right to this information."

I hear these words in many places, from many people and from documents with information erased and hidden. Ultimately, it makes me stronger. I begin to question the clerks who say they cannot show me things. My voice no longer shakes. "Why should you be allowed to see information about me that I'm not allowed to see?" I ask. "Does that make sense to you? Does it seem fair?"

"It's not up to us," the clerks say, their body language asking me to leave quietly.

But I am not done. "If you can see it, and I can't, to me that's an invasion of my privacy."

"We have to follow these policies," they say, blaming their inability to help me on others. They cite me rules and regulations. "These were created to protect you," they say.

"I do not want protection," I tell them. "I want to know where I came from. I am a human being, just like you. Stand in my shoes."

I become bold, thorough. I keep records of every place I visit, every document I see. Ultimately, I replace my skinny file folder with a large binder, one that is three inches thick with extra-strong rings. But, despite the volume of information I gather, months pass, then years, and I do not find my birth family. I am discouraged and decide to put my search on hold for a while.

Jon and I marry, and the day after our wedding, we leave California on a tandem bicycle, our destination a college in central Massachusetts where he is the new president.

A box inside our moving van carries my binder full of papers and documents, my breadcrumbs from the forest floor. I leave the state of my birth, but I have not given up trying to find my way home.

23

We ride our tandem bike right up to the front door of the college president's house in Worcester, Massachusetts. I look at the beautifully landscaped yard, the house with the columned porch, and think about the garage I lived in when I was rowing in Long Beach. I look at Jon and shrug. "I guess we'll just have to make do."

Mom thinks the notion of me being a college president's wife is as frightening as me trying to be a brain surgeon. "Don't spill anything,.."

Her concern is validated when I host my first official tea. I borrow a silver tea service from a neighbor who neglects to tell me that when her niece broke off the ornate ball on top of the tea pot, she reattached it with a small wad of bubble gum. As I pour a cup of tea for the first woman in line, the silver ball tumbles off the pot right into the woman's cup, a pink gob of bubble gum trailing behind like a kite tail. The woman I'm serving does not even crack a smile, saying simply, "I would prefer coffee."

A blizzard rages on the night we host a reception honoring major donors to the college. Minutes before the guests are to arrive, I decide to light the logs in the fireplace, hoping to make the living room warm and inviting. I never think to check the flue. Pine boughs make a fast fire and a lot of smoke. Within seconds, every fire alarm in the house is blaring and a thick cloud of smoke cloaks everything from the ceiling to our waists as we race around, opening windows and fanning out smoke with copies of *National Geographic*. The first guest arrives just after we close the last window. When she enters, she breathes in deeply. "What a lovely smokey smell. It's so homey."

I smile broadly. A homey feel was my intention exactly.

Despite these transgressions, and others, the college allows us to stay. And despite the thirty-five hundred mile distance from Lafayette, I begin my search anew.

I reread every letter that was exchanged between my parents and the adoption agency, searching for new clues, anything I might have missed. Reading them, I step into my parents shoes in the 1950's, under the microscope of county adoption agencies. Their first application to the County of Los Angeles Bureau of Adoptions was denied.

> Dear Mr. and Mrs. Sacconaghi:
> We received a letter from the Catholic Welfare
> Bureau informing us that you cannot be approved..."

Dad was a Catholic, Mom a Presbyterian, and a 'mixed marriage' was not considered a proper environment for children. Mom and Dad's neighbors appealed to the Catholic Welfare Bureau on their behalf. "In our opinion, the Sacconaghi's are very fine people..." they wrote. "Louie is very fond of children and my daughter is especially fond of Betty, even referring to her as Aunt Betty. I am sure they would be an ideal mother and father to any child..."

The Bureau ultimately reversed it's decision and Mom and Dad were able to adopt Frankie. But then they moved north, hundreds of miles away, to a different county where social workers and neighbors knew nothing about them. Mom was thirty-four, Dad, forty-three, and time was not on their side to adopt a second child.

For my mother, raised in a small Ohio town where everyone knew everyone, being judged by strangers as to her fitness to parent must have been excruciating. I read the forms she had to fill out, the questions she had to answer. We will talk about all of this someday, I think. She will tell me what it was like to go through this.

But even without speaking to her, I can see for myself, the process, the ordeal. She dutifully mailed in a photostatic copy of her marriage certificate, a physician's statement attesting to their infertility problems, a verification of Dad's employment, a form from the local Catholic Church stating that Dad was a practicing Catholic.

She was asked to write about why she wanted to adopt a second child. I imagine Mom wanted to write a single sentence. "BECAUSE I LOVE CHILDREN AND WANT TO RAISE A FAMILY!" Instead, she wrote a thoughtful, appropriate response, stuck a three cent stamp on the envelope, and sent it in, receiving a form letter in reply stating that the agency would need to interview them to gain "a fuller understanding" of their request.

The interview was in March. Mom marked the date in the small pocket calendar she kept in her billfold, the one with a drawing of a little blonde-haired girl on the cover. A month later, the calendar shows that on April 12th, Mom had her hair done at the Towne and Country Hair Salon in Walnut Creek. She had no idea that a baby born that day would become her daughter.

In May, Mom and Dad passed muster and the agency moved forward with their application. In June, on their tenth wedding anniversary, the phone rang. "We have a baby in mind for you," a social worker said, but before Mom could find out if it was a boy or a girl, Frankie pushed down the switchhook, cutting the phone connection. "It's a girl," the social worker told Mom when she called back. But more paperwork was required. The baby had allergies and was considered high risk. Another month passed before Mom received the phone call. "You can come and take your daughter home."

The moment the social worker placed me in her arms, she became my mother and I became her daughter. During the drive home, she held me on her lap while Frankie romped on the scratchy upholstery of the old Dodge station. When Dad pulled into the driveway on La Cañada Road, at the age of three months and five days, I was finally home. But my parents were not done jumping through hoops yet. The adoption, as was common practice, wasn't finalized for another year and there were scheduled visits by a social worker. It wasn't until July of 1956 that they were given a document which declared:

...CECILIA ANNE PORTER, is hereby adopted by petitioners LOUIE B. and BETTY L. SACCONAGHI... and (will) be henceforth known as JEAN ANNE SACCONAGHI.

I examine this document and others. I spend hours moving pieces of paper around on the dining room table as if I am assembling a giant jigsaw puzzle, trying to figure out what fits where, and to see what I can try next. I send away for Xeroxed pages of city directories, for copies of marriage certificates, for alumni lists from schools. Rejections of requests take me weeks to get over. Some days, I am too exhausted to open an envelope.

I don't even notice it at first. I send money to the Multnomah County Library to Xerox the page of "Porters" in the Portland City Directory of 1954. I am looking for my maternal grandfather who was listed as a chicken farmer. When the page arrives, I look through all the Porters and don't find a single farmer. I never think to look for a secretary.

Weeks later, I scan the page again and think to check, and while there isn't a single secretary listed, there is a Porter who was a stenographer.

Lenore C. Porter.

I stare at the entry. Could the "C" stand for Cecilia? But it is her place of employment that trips my heart: she was a stenographer at the medical school. My birth father was purportedly a medical student. Have I at long last found my birth mother?

I try to get her employment records from the medical school. I try to get marriage records for Lenore C. Porter from the State of Oregon. I look for Lenore C. Porters in endless phone books. Nothing. I am stuck. I think about calling my old professor, John Riley, in Los Angeles to see if he has any new ideas. But then something happens that makes me stop searching altogether.

24

I am pregnant. I cannot wait to tell my mom. A grandchild, her first grandchild! I decide to tell her in person and fly home to California a few days before Christmas to announce the news. On board the plane, I fantasize about how I will tell her and what her reaction will be, about how she will be right there with me in the delivery room. I ring her doorbell and grin when she opens the door. "I've got something to tell you," I say, giving her a big hug.

"I've got something to tell you too," she says, stopping me before I say a word. As she holds my hand tightly in the entryway, I look into her eyes and feel the blood drain from my face. "I have cancer," says Mom. "It doesn't look good."

Words fail me. We hug for a long time, neither one of us saying a word, until I remember my news. "You're going to be a grandmother." She hugs me even harder, so happy for her tomboy daughter who refused to play with dolls, who used Betsy Wetsy for target practice, who still has to read a cookbook in order to scramble eggs, who has never changed a diaper. A mother! We don't cry in the entryway. We laugh.

She doesn't know her prognosis yet. Her doctor is old-fashioned. "Let's do all the tests first." I take her to the hospital for a cat scan and while I am waiting, I buy her a stuffed bear at the hospital store. I have never bought her anything like this before, a child's toy, and I'm not sure she'll want it, she'll think I'm just being silly. But her face melts when I give it to her and I see a glimpse of my mother as a child as she tucks the light brown bear in with her under the thermal blanket on the gurney. The little bear will be with her all the way through this journey.

We have only ten weeks.

I am with Mom when she is finally told the truth: she is dying. The doctor leaves the room and we become rivers of grief, for as long as Mom can stand it, all of three minutes maybe, and then she is cracking jokes again. She will not survive the day if she takes this dying thing too seriously. "Well," she says, "I wouldn't have been a lot of help anyway since I never gave birth."

I don't laugh. "Giving birth doesn't have anything to do with being a good mother." She is my mentor, my friend. How can I be a good mother without her?

Frankie must be told. I reach him by phone at an old hotel where he rents a room and tell him our mother is very ill. "Yeah?" he says. "Tell her I need some money."

"Frankie... Mom's dying."

There is a short pause, then he says, "Do you have any money?"

I agree to meet him at the BART station near Mom's townhouse. I haven't seen him in three years, but he is easy to recognize, dressed all in black. "Frank!" I call, waving.

He walks briskly toward me. "How much did you bring?" I hand him five twenties. "This is it?"

"It's all she had in her wallet."

"Shit."

"Frankie, don't you understand? Mom's dying."

"Well, I need more than this."

I am unsure how to read his angry face. Does he not comprehend or does he not care? "Do you want to see her?"

"No." My brother spits on his hand and leans down to rub a scuff mark on one of his black boots. "I think I've caused her enough trouble," he says without looking up.

"You sure? I don't know how much time she has."

He shrugs as he pockets the money. "Can't you give me more than this?"

I shake my head and he spins on his heel without saying goodbye, disappearing into the BART station. He does not call again.

"I want you to promise me," Mom says that night. "When I'm gone, you are not to become responsible for him. I don't him to be your burden, especially with the baby on the way." She looks at me sternly. "Promise."

"Okay." It is an easy promise to make.

I drive her to the appointment with her new oncologist, and afterward, pull the doctor aside. "Back in Massachusetts, I heard my baby's heartbeat for the first time." It was a magical. "Is there any way I could arrange for my mom to hear her grandchild's heartbeat?"

The doctor clears his throat and looks away. I realize it is not easy being the doctor of a patient who is going to die. There are tears in his eyes when he looks back. "I think we can do something better than that."

We are not supposed to tell anyone what the doctor is letting us do because I do not belong to the hospital's HMO. It is very hush-hush as I push Mom in a wheelchair to the ultrasound room. The doctor is an angel disguised in a white jacket. He cannot make her cancer go away. But he can do this.

I lie on the table with slippery gel on my belly and a probe cold against my skin. Mom holds my hand as we watch the ultrasound monitor and see, all grainy and black and white, my baby, my mother's first grandchild. We cannot tell if it is a boy or a girl as it holds its thumb to its mouth, moving in rapid, jerky motions. We laugh, enchanted. This is a brilliant child, a gifted child. Mom does not say she feels sorry for herself that this is the closest she will get to the delivery room. She says, "Wow!"

I stare at the screen, torn between joy and anguish, remembering the other baby, the one I wasn't ready for. Mom knows nothing about my abortion many years before, but I have never forgotten. At the same time my mother and I are looking at the baby she will never get to hold, I am remembering a choice made long ago. We both cry.

Pushing her in the wheelchair back to the doctor's office, I end up turning down the wrong hall and we find ourselves at the window of the hospital nursery. On the other side of the window is a single baby. The candy-striper inside thinks we are family and pushes the bassinet closer so we can have a look.

Taped to the side of the plexiglass bassinet is a little white card that says:

Hi! I'm a boy! My name is Robert.
I weigh 10 pounds 0 ounces.

We stare at the sleeping newborn as if he has been magically transported here from the ultrasound screen. Mom reaches back and grabs my hand and without taking her eyes off the baby says, "You're going to have a beautiful son like that for Jon."

"You saw him first Mom," I whisper. "Before anybody."

Less than two weeks later, the pain in her abdomen is so intense she has to crawl on her hands and knees to get into the back seat of her white Chevy Nova so I can drive her to the hospice. When the doctor sees her, he tells me it will only be a matter of hours. He promises to try to make her comfortable, and she slips into a coma, morphine dripping into her arm.

I call Jon. He is shocked at how quickly Mom is slipping away and promises to fly out from Massachusetts as soon as he can, on Friday. When I get off the phone, I sit and talk to my mother, even though she is asleep and cannot hear me. "Let go," I tell her as I hold her hand, stroking it gently. "I don't want you to hurt anymore. Jon is coming Friday. Lue and Margaret and Linda and Jackie are here. I'm not alone."

But Mom does not die in a few hours like the doctor predicted. She might be in a coma, but I believe she knows what I have said. She is waiting for Jon.

I stand in the doorway of her room at two in the morning and watch as her chest rises and falls with each breath. On the nightstand beside her bed is a photograph of her parents and one of Dad, grinning his Vince Lombardi grin. They are with me in this room on this deathwatch.

I think about the secrets between us. She is my best friend, my mother, and I want to get rid of the secrets, to confess. "I was searching Mom." I need to know. "Is that okay?" But it is too late to tell her this, to ask her this. Her eyes are covered with gauze patches to keep them from drying out. She can no longer look into my eyes and tell me how she feels. She cannot squeeze my hand and give me permission to do what I need to do, nor can she ask me to leave the breadcrumbs where they are. This is the cost of my burglary. I will never know how my mother would feel about my desire to unearth my roots. I will never have a deep conversation with her about the bond that made us mother and daughter. I will regret this, always.

For five days and nights, I do not move from the cot by her bed. Every day the hospice nurses tell me it is only a matter of hours. Every day, Mom hangs on, her chest rising and falling. Jon arrives, and still her rattled breathing continues. I know why. She does not want me in this room, holding her hand. She does not think I will survive her death intact. This is not, after all, like her arriving home twenty minutes late. She is leaving forever.

Jon pries me away after midnight. "You're exhausted," he says. "You have think about the baby. What will it do to your mom if you get sick and miscarry the baby."

We are only in Mom's townhouse for an hour when the hospital calls at three in the morning. "She's gone."

I stand at the foot of her bed and look at her body one last time. I have heard that when you're dying, your whole life can flash before your eyes. It can happen for the living, too. As I stand there, knowing I will never see her again, it runs through my mind like a movie: the spoonfuls of brown sugar in the dark; sitting on the kitchen counter as she puts Bactine and Band-Aids on my scraped knees; sitting on her lap at a campfire at Feather River, my head against her chest as her heart beats in rhythm to "I've Been Working On The Railroad"; her face as the helicopter rose up into the air; her stroking her father's hand the last day she saw him; her calmness that night long ago with a knife at her throat; her hugging Jon at our wedding; her joy at seeing the baby on the ultrasound.

My first sentence ever was, "Mommy where are you." I am thirty-two years old and the question is on my lips in this room. Where are you now

Mom? Was it scary? Is there an afterlife? I stand over her body in disbelief. Betty Wenger Sacconaghi can't be gone, just like that, her chest has been rising and falling my whole life, it cannot stop.

But it has. Her cheek is cold to my touch. She is not here anymore, even though her body lies before me, her hands clutching the honeysuckle flowers Margaret brought her yesterday. The flowers make the room smell like Hawaii. Mom got to go to Hawaii once. She liked to travel, to have adventures. Her room smells of adventure. She would like this. Under her arm is the teddy bear I bought for her at the hospital store. It makes me feel better to know she didn't die alone.

The nurse at the hospice tells me to go home and cry. No one at the hospice has seen me cry. But the tears won't come. They don't come when Margaret and Lue help me pack up Mom's things a few days later. They don't even come when I scatter her ashes in San Francisco Bay in the shadow of the Golden Gate Bridge. They don't come for six whole months, until the day I give birth to a nearly ten pound baby boy, just like Mom told me I would.

When I hold him in my arms, it is the first time in my life I have ever seen anyone I am biologically related to. This is a very profound thing, but I am not ready to think about it yet. I have been waiting to cry.

I wake up in the hospital at three o'clock in the morning, my newborn son tucked in beside my bed, sleeping. Taped to the side of his plexiglass bassinet is a white card.

Hi! I'm a boy! My name is Kristoffer.
I weigh 9 pounds 15 ½ ounces.

I watch as his chest rises and falls.

Suddenly the tears come, not in waves, but in an unrelenting flood. A nurse slips into the room and holds my hand for awhile, saying nothing, as if she knows there is nothing to say. I cannot stop the wracking sobs, even after there are no tears left. In my arms is Mom's teddy bear. We are going to go on this journey together.

25

Tiff is the nickname we give our son Kristoffer, and he is an enchanting child, a brilliant child. While Jon reads him a cartoon in the newspaper, Tiff takes a bite out of the funnies section. This is his first solid food.

I watch from across the room, thinking how Mom should be here to laugh at the tiny bite in the edge of the newspaper. It is the moment I decide. "I'm never going to search again."

Mom has been gone for over a year and during that time, I haven't mentioned my search once. Jon looks up while Tiff tries a bite of the sportspage. "What?"

"I've decided I'm not going to search for my birth family anymore." I don't say it's too disloyal or I have no right to do this or what was I thinking of all those years. I just say, "I'm done."

Jon takes the paper out of Tiff's mouth. "I think you ought to give it one more try," he says as he puts the paper out of reach.

"It's impossible to do anything from this distance."

"Then hire a private investigator."

Have I brought this up simply for his encouragement? Am I just asking for his permission to begin again? Mom loved Jon. "I think you should just do it," he says. I let him speak for her.

"Okay."

Through a friend, I get the phone number of Sheila Klopper, a private investigator in the Bay Area. Not only is Sheila a detective, she is also an adoptee. She sounds like the perfect choice and I call her from Massachusetts. But, after listening to me describe everything I have tried and everything I know, she does not sound very hopeful.

"It seems to me the only lead really worth following is on this Lenore C. Porter, but I'll be honest with you. It sounds like your birth mother got married right after you were born. She's been living under a different name ever since. Even if this Lenore C. Porter is who you're looking for, she won't be easy to find through normal channels."

"Aren't there other ways to get information?" I've been going through normal channels for years.

"Like what?"

"I don't know. Borrowing files without permission?"

"We don't do that kind of thing. That only happens on television."

"Oh." I had hoped that, like Simon and Simon or Magnum P.I., a hired investigator would sneak into the county hospital late at night and get my birth mother's medical record, that the hospital supervisor would gnash her teeth in the morning when she discovered the open drawer, the empty file. This has been my fantasy. "Ha! Ha! Ha!" I would say to the supervisor. "I found her!"

For the first time since I began searching, I give up. I know I'll never learn the identity of my birth parents, I'll never know anything about my family tree. My roots were turned under long ago. My search is over.

All I anticipate receiving from the detective is a bill for services rendered, so when the phone rings on a hot and humid night in July, she is the last person I expect to hear on the line. "Jean? It's Sheila Klopper. You'd better sit down. I've found your birth mother."

I sink down onto the bed. "What?"

"I've found your birth mother."

I heard her the first time, but I almost say "what?" again, just to hear her say the words once more. She's found my birth mother? She's found my birth mother!

Sheila explains. She had requested a marriage record from the state of Oregon (through normal channels) for anyone named Lenore C. Porter who married between April of 1955 and December of 1956. Only one certificate came up. The marriage certificate arrived in the mail this afternoon and the information it contains is everything we need to know.

Lenore C. Porter's full name is Lenore *Cecilia* Porter. She was born on

August 10, 1934, in Portland, Oregon. There is no doubt in my mind, or in Sheila's, that we have found, on the slimmest of leads, the right person.

But where is she now? In June of 1955, only seven weeks after my birth, Lenore Porter married a man named Louis Iacarella from Minnesota. After checking Oregon information and finding no Iacarellas, Sheila tries Minnesota. Twenty-six Iacarellas are listed. She calls the first one on the list, a cousin of Lou's, who tells her that Lenore and Lou divorced years ago, that Lou has since passed away, and Lenore now lives in Richland, Washington.

She then tells Sheila something else, something extraordinary: the names of Lenore's seven children, Mary, Mike, Sue, Jim, Cathy, Bob and Charles, my brothers and sisters. "What do you want to do?" Sheila asks me on the phone. "How do you want to handle this?"

For the first time in my life, I have the ability to contact the woman who gave birth to me. What should I do? During five years of searching, I haven't spent any time planning for this moment. It seemed too much to hope for, and now that it's arrived, I am not prepared. How do you break the news to a stranger, a stranger who gave birth to you, that you'd like to hear their voice, to see their face?

Sheila and Jon and I talk over what options there might be. We know Lenore is Catholic. She listed this on both the information sheet she filled out in 1955 and later when she wrote the agency to inquire whether I had been adopted by a Catholic family. So, with Jon and Sheila's help, I decide to call the Catholic parish in Richland, Washington. I introduce myself to the priest who answers the phone, and ask, "Is there a woman named Lenore Iacarella in your parish?"

"Yes," the priest responds.

I explain the situation. "I don't want her to be alone when she receives this information. I want her to have someone to support her and I also want her to know that if she doesn't want any contact from me, that's okay."

The priest is very nice and agrees to contact her and then call me back.

Less than five minutes later, my phone rings. "Call her," he says. "She's been looking for you for years."

Jon takes Tiff from my arms to tuck him into bed and I am alone. What am I going to say? She's waiting. Three thousand miles away, the woman who gave birth to me is waiting by a phone.

With no idea what I am going to say, I pick up the phone and dial.

The mother can look back now and see the moment clearly. She lost the two babies, first Geraldine, born a month premature, living only a day, then Angela, who was born dead, and there were no more babies after that, as if her body was telling her to stop, that it could do no more. And then the obsession began.

She needed another baby, just one more, and her solution was perfect: they would adopt a baby girl. It would be like getting Cecilia back.

But her husband did not understand. He was happy with their seven children. Why did she need another child, one that wasn't even theirs? They argued. He finally agreed to go with her to the adoption agency, but during the interview he told the social worker that he loved his family the way it was, he had only come along to mollify his wife.

She felt betrayed. It was the moment the marriage ended for her. Ultimately, she left him and moved west to marry another man, a marriage that also didn't last. She can look back now, years later, and see how she'd ripped her children in half, and the insanity of it all. She can see that she'd needed help, that her obsession, her melancholy, had nothing to do with her husband or their marriage, but it was too late to change all that had happened.

There are so many things in her life she wishes she could do over.

But she is happy now, dating a man who empathizes with her losses, her mistakes, a man who lost his own children through divorce. She told him about Cecilia the very first day they met. She has told many people about her firstborn child. Even her other children now know about their lost sister.

When the phone rings during dinner, she is surprised to hear the priest's voice. His words make her feel fear. "Your daughter would like to speak to you."

For an instant, she thinks something has happened back home in Minnesota, that one of the girls is trying to reach her. But that doesn't make any sense. Her children know her phone number. If there's an emergency they would just call her directly. Her mind races. "Your daughter would like to speak to you." And she realizes.

Cecilia.

She wants to scream. She does scream. "Oh my god!" A euphoria fills her unlike anything she has ever felt.

air

My Family Tree

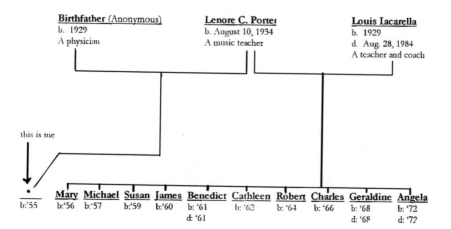

	Birthfather (Anonymous)	Lenore C. Porter	Louis Iacarella
	b. 1929	b. August 10, 1934	b. 1929
	A physician	A music teacher	d. Aug. 28, 1984
			A teacher and coach

this is me

_____	Mary	Michael	Susan	James	Benedict	Cathleen	Robert	Charles	Geraldine	Angela
b:'55	b:'56	b:'57	b:'59	b:'60	b: '61	b: '62	b: '64	b: '66	b: '68	b: '72
					d: '61				d: '68	d: '72

26

I press the numbers on the phone, my heart pounding in my chest. The phone rings once, then a woman answers. "Hello?" For the first time, I hear my birth mother's voice. It is timid and soft, like Jackie Kennedy and Marilyn Monroe all rolled into one.

What should I say? "Lenore?"

"Cecilia?" Her voice tells me she is shaking.

"Well, Jean. My parents named me Jean."

"My god." I can feel her tears even though I cannot see her face. "I don't believe this is happening."

"I don't either." A rush of adrenaline hits me. I am Columbus sighting land.

"Just before you called, I spoke to my daughter Sue on the phone, and she's so excited. You have seven brothers and sisters."

"Incredible," is all I can think of to say.

"There are so many things I want to know, so many questions I want to ask." I can tell by her voice: my birth mother is happy I have called. She wants to know what happened. I have worried that I would be intruding, but I instantly know I have done the right thing.

So we begin. I came out of her body, yet until now, she didn't even know my name. We are strangers, intimate strangers.

I go first. "My parents were wonderful." I tell her about Mom and Dad and the house on La Cañada Road. I tell her I always knew I was adopted. "Mom told me the agency said it was very hard for you to give me up. She gave me the baby dress you bought me. I still have it."

"Baby dress?" My birth mother's voice hesitates. "I didn't give you a dress."

We both pause. Have I made a mistake? Is this really my birth mother?

But the dates fit, the names fit. I haven't made a mistake, the agency just told a white lie to be nice. They told more than one lie to be nice. "There wasn't any opportunity for me to buy you anything," my birth mother explains. "The last time I saw you was the day I left the hospital. You were three days old. I remember it like it was yesterday." And her story tumbles out, water from a broken dam.

"You were the result of a single date." He was a medical student she knew casually. She wasn't 'that kind of girl', but she had a couple of beers and didn't normally drink and it just happened. "I didn't know I was pregnant for months. The first doctor I went to told me I had an infection and he cauterized my cervix. It wasn't until two months later that a different doctor told me the truth. I was pregnant. When I told him what the first doctor had done, he said, 'my dear, that gentleman was just trying to help you by aborting your baby.'"

I have a fleeting image of Tiff's ultrasound. My god.

Lenore continues. "I was adopted too, and I had always promised myself that what happened to my own mother was never going to happen to me. So when I learned I was pregnant, I was devastated.

"Telling my parents was one of the worst moments of my life. It was right before Christmas. My mother cried, but my father, he didn't say anything. I loved him so much and he just stared at me. I wanted to die."

I imagine this grim holiday long ago, with my heart beating inside her, causing so much pain.

"I called the young man responsible and he asked, 'how do you know it was me.' I told him I wasn't with anyone else, and then he said, 'but how do *I* know it was me.' I never heard from him again.

"No one was to know. My parents sent me to Seattle, to a home for unwed pregnant girls. It was also a home for the elderly and infirm and over. the doorway was a sign that said, ENTER YE INTO THE TWILIGHT OF YOUR LIFE. I felt like it was my twilight. They assigned me a bed in a room full of elderly women. One of them died that first night and I was so terrified, I just ran. I got to the bus depot and called friends of my parents who lived in California. I didn't know where else to turn. They said I could stay with them, so I got on a Greyhound Bus and arrived in Martinez the next day without even a suitcase.

"There was never any question about what I would do. I would put my baby up for adoption. I went to church every day and prayed for forgiveness. I have to be honest, I just wanted it to be over. I signed those papers and waited for you to be born so I could get on with my life.

"The week you were due, I was walking home from Mass and this man came out of nowhere, grabbing me from behind. He was from a nearby facility for mentally ill people, and as he choked me, I screamed, 'My baby! My baby!' People ran to help and I felt them lifting him off me.

"That was the second time someone tried to kill you." She pauses. "But you were meant to be born. I went into labor after that. The pains were horrible. I'd never had the process of giving birth explained to me, so I was very afraid. I thought I was going to die. I lay there staring at those bright delivery room lights until they finally put me out.

"They told me I had a baby girl and I asked to see you. That's when it happened. No one told me how I would feel after you were born. As soon as I held you in my arms, I knew I couldn't give you up.

"I called my parents and begged them to let me bring you home. My father said if I kept you, I'd never be allowed back in their house. I wanted to take you and run, but where would I go? You weren't even legally mine. I had already signed the papers.

"A social worker came for you when you were three days old. I can still see the taillights of her car disappearing around the corner. And you were gone."

I am thirty-three years old and finally know how I came into being. Lenore's words are spackle, filling empty spaces inside me.

"I returned to Oregon, to my parent's house, and my mother introduced me to this handsome new school teacher in town. He called the first night I was home and asked me out. He was a wonderful guy, a very nice man, and after just a few dates, my parents asked him his intentions. He proposed to me within a week, on May Day."

Wait a minute. The first of May? I was born on April 12th. She was engaged to be married less than three weeks later to a man she'd just met?

"Yes," Lenore says. "Seven weeks after you were born, I was walking down the aisle. I didn't really fall in love with Lou as much as the idea that my parents might forgive me. My fantasy was that by getting married, they would be proud of me again. Lou knew the truth. A priest told him I was a fallen woman before our wedding. But he loved me, and I grew to love him.

"I was told to forget about you. I played the game. I never mentioned you and acted like nothing had ever happened. But deep inside was this incredible pain. I'd just lost my child. I wasn't ready for anything, certainly not marriage and certainly not a family.

"When our first child, Mary, was born the next summer, I thought I'd finally get over you, but it just made it worse. When she learned to walk, to talk, when she'd hug me tight, it made me know all the more what I'd lost.

"It affected my marriage. I felt sad and Lou couldn't make the sadness go away. Sometimes I felt my unhappiness was because of him. But it wasn't Lou. It was me."

I think about my sister Mary, born just fourteen months after me, so close to my wake. This cost her, cost them all. Lenore and Lou never had a chance for a normal marriage - because of me.

Lenore gasps. "Sue! Jean, I almost forgot. I told her I'd have you call her right away. You just have to, she's so excited."

I am not ready for this first conversation with my birth mother to end, but we promise to talk again the next day. I depress the switchhook and immediately dial my sister's number.

27

"Hello?" This is my sister's voice.

"Sue. I'm your sister, Jean." It feels wonderful to say this.

"Oh my god. The hair on my arms is standing straight up. I never thought this would happen."

"Me either."

"Welcome to the family."

I wish I could hug her through the phone. After all the people who made me feel like my desire to find my birth family was wrong, I'm invited in their door, just like that. "I always wanted to have a big family."

"Well get ready," she says, laughing. "There are a lot of us." I learn that she's known about me since she was sixteen. "Mom took me aside and told me I had an older sister she'd given up for adoption, and I wasn't shocked. I always knew something was wrong, something was missing. I felt angry for not knowing you, and I wondered if you were dead or alive. I saw a segment on *Sixty Minutes* about a boy who was murdered by his adopted parents, and I wondered if something like that had happened to you."

It makes me feel strange that this was the image she had of me and my family. "I had great parents, a great neighborhood to grow up in."

"Did you ever think about us?" she asks. "I always thought about you on your birthday, at Christmas. I knew you were out there, somewhere, and I wondered if you were happy."

"I was, Sue. I was happy."

We talk and talk until my *sister* says, "You've got to call Bobby and Charlie. They're waiting for you."

I have brothers named Bobby and Charlie! I dial their number in Los Angeles. "Hey Jean. It's your brother Bob." He's a photographer, Charlie, an actor. Their voices say, 'pull up a chair and tell us what you've been up to.' I have been loved in absentia. I never expected this kind of welcome, ever. It is so easy to talk to them. After a half hour, Charlie says, "You've got to call Cathy in Minneapolis."

"Jean!" Cathy shouts. "It's about time you called." She scolds me as if I have been out late. A half hour later, she says, "You gotta call Jim. I know it's late, but you just gotta call him."

Jim is laughing when he answers the phone. "I figured by the time my sisters stopped talking to you it would be tomorrow." Apparently he looks at his clock, because he laughs again. "Oh. I guess it *is* tomorrow."

At two in the morning, when I put down the phone, I have spoken to all my brothers and sisters except the two oldest ones, Mary and Mike. My hand lingers on the earpiece. It is warm to the touch. I have been talking to my family. My dream has come true. I *am* the oldest member of a Brady Bunch. I envision pillow fights and slumber parties and trips to Disneyland.

The next morning I talk to Mary and instantly feel an affinity for her. We are closest in age, just fourteen months apart. "We were supposed to be a pair," she says. "Mike had Jim, Sue had Cathy, and Bob had Charlie. I was supposed to have you."

"I wish I'd known you," I say. "All of you."

"When I heard you called Mom, I almost fell over. You see, last week, I prayed to find you. I got down on my knees with my children and we prayed that you would be found. So I couldn't believe it when Sue called me. It was surreal."

I have been prayed for, wanted, and accepted without paying an ounce of dues. It's overwhelming.

I leave a message for my oldest brother, Mike, on his answering machine, but he doesn't call back. A couple days later, I try again. Still nothing. Just a year younger than Mary, he doesn't seem thrilled by my arrival. A week passes. I try his number yet again, and this time get a person instead of a machine. "Mike?"

His voice is hesitant. "Yeah?"

"Hey, it's Jean. I thought I'd call and introduce myself."

His voice remains guarded, but before long we are talking about everything from sports to high school marching bands. I had intended this to be a brief phone call, just to break the ice, but it stretches to over an hour and our conversation drifts to a more serious topic: us.

Mike is up-front about his feelings. "I've been angry. It was embarrassing to learn that my mom got pregnant before she met my dad. I'm not trying to make you feel bad, just to have you understand, that's how I've been seeing this. I've had no desire to talk to you."

"It's okay Mike. There are no 'have to's' here. We don't have to have a relationship."

"I know," he says. "But I've got a feeling now you're going to be a part of my life forever."

With one phone call, I feel completely at ease with him, as if I have known him my whole life. I embrace Mike, and all my brothers and sisters. I do not think about Frankie at all. I have found my real brothers and sisters.

I do not think about Frankie once.

28

It happens because of words spoken over the phone, because of thirty-three years apart, and because we are on terra incognita.

My birth mother and I spend hours becoming acquainted over the phone. We cannot see each other's eyes, so I do not see her reaction when I tell her the sentence I have waited to say ever since I began searching. I do not see what the words do to her. "I always wanted to find you to tell you that you did the right thing when you put me up for adoption." I believe hearing this will make her feel good.

"No, I didn't." There is a razor edge to her voice. "I should have taken you and run!"

I am not expecting anger and stumble, unsure of what to say next. "I just meant that everything worked out okay."

"It's not okay when people lie to you. The social worker promised me you were going to your new home the very day I gave you up, but you weren't placed for three months."

"Well, that was just because I had some allergies, and..."

"Don't you see? I was married when you were less than two months old. I could have come back for you. I *would* have come back for you. All these years we should have been together."

I flash on my mom and my stomach hurts at the thought of someone erasing my childhood with her.

"They weren't supposed to change your name. And you were supposed to be baptized right away, and they didn't do that either."

They? She is talking about my parents.

Emotions flood into my veins. Some of them are new to me. I don't even have names for them. "I had great parents," I say, trying to keep my voice calm. "They loved me very much."

"*I* loved you," Lenore says.

A knee-jerk reaction inside me, like a baby kicking. She loved me? She doesn't even *know* me. This emotion I am feeling - is this what rage feels like?

I end our phone conversation as soon as it's polite, and go to check on Tiff in his crib. It is late, and I stop in front of the photograph of my parents hanging in the hallway.

"I loved you." Lenore's words echo inside as I stare at the photograph. I was eight when this picture was taken at a party, Dad's arm around Mom's waist, her head resting on his shoulder. I take them with me now as I go to bed, hugging them in my arms. It is a long time before I fall asleep.

The next day, an overnight package arrives from Lenore containing an eight by ten black and white glossy photograph of her. I see my birth mother's face for the first time. She is wearing a wig and makeup and a nice smile and does not look anything like I expected. I do not think she looks like me.

She receives a similar package of photographs from me and calls to let me know. "We look like twins," she says. I lie on the bed and stare at the ceiling. I do not feel like talking to her anymore.

What is happening?

The initial fireworks excitement I felt dissolves into awkward feelings. Yet, it doesn't make sense, my unforgiving attitude, my desire for distance. After all, I am the one who searched for her, and Lenore has been honest and forthcoming, answering every difficult question I pose.

"Who was my birth father?"

Without a moment's hesitation she reveals his identity. Information I already have leads me directly to him, and I call Lenore to let her know, "I'm planning to write him a letter and I'll let you know if I hear back." I believe it's her right to know this, that she'll appreciate my candor. Instantly, I know I have made a mistake.

"I've got to go," Lenore says, her voice breaking into a sob. She calls me later and says she's been crying non-stop. "He has no right to know you. He abandoned us both. I didn't realize how angry I was at him until now."

I feel awful that Lenore has been crying. I was just trying to be honest and open, and instead I have hurt her, and I never meant to hurt her. But because she's angry at him, does that mean I have to be angry also? He hurt her horribly, but he is my birth father. I have searched to find answers, not to pass judgments. But aren't I passing judgments on Lenore? "I'm sorry," I say. "I'm sorry I hurt you."

"I just want to clutch you to my breast," she says, "and make these awful feelings disappear."

Her words are too intimate, too needy. I cannot be the baby she gave away. I am not Cecilia nor do I want to be.

It happens because of words said over a telephone. It happens because my mother is dead and I have opened the door to a woman who wants to take her place, a woman who gave birth to me.

Less than a week after I find my birth mother, I close the door to my heart and barricade it with the heaviest furniture I can find. It will be a long time before I understand why.

29

I am afraid.

My birth mother and I are meeting face-to-face in Minneapolis on what will be her 54th birthday. Everyone in the family will be on hand for the reunion, including Bobby and Charlie who are flying in from Los Angeles. I am so excited, I can't sleep, but I am also afraid of the unknown, of what to say to the woman who gave birth to me, and of the angry feelings I have toward her that will not go away. The plane ticket I have to Minneapolis is taking me into uncharted territory.

Having a national magazine cover the event isn't helping. Just two days after I first phoned Lenore, Sue calls. "Did you hear what Charlie is trying do? Get us on *Donahue* or *Oprah*. I told him he better not agree to anything without talking to you first."

I think about all the times during my search when I read about other reunions and how the stories gave me hope and kept me from giving up. I don't mind the idea of sharing our story, but how will Lenore feel? Surprisingly, she welcomes the idea.

People Magazine agrees to do an exclusive story on our reunion, but this is all arranged before these awkward feelings set in. What kind of article will my meeting Lenore make now? Reunions are supposed to be fairytales, fantasies fulfilled. What is happening between us is too confusing for me to understand, much less articulate. My emotions are all over the map.

A reporter flies to Worcester to interview me. I tell him all about my mom, Betty, and about my warm and welcoming new brothers and sisters. I tell him that I have just learned I'm pregnant with my second child, that the due date is my own birthday. "I feel like I am living inside a movie."

"You must be so excited to meet your birth mother," he says.

"Of course," I say, even though excitement is not really the emotion I am feeling.

The reporter had interviewed Lenore before me, and she told him she was elated she could finally tell the world the truth. "I don't have seven children, I have eight. Count 'em. I will never again have to mentally subtract one whenever someone asks 'how many children do you have'."

When the reporter tells me this, it does not make me feel elated. It makes me feel like I am cheating on my mother. If Lenore now has 'eight' children, where does that leave my mom?

I do not sleep the night before the reunion. I watch the red numbers on the alarm clock move slowly toward dawn, counting the minutes until I meet my seven brothers and sisters. I am excited.

I am also meeting the woman who gave birth to me. I am afraid.

Before leaving for the airport, I retrieve Mom's wedding ring from my jewelry box, and slip it onto my ring finger beside my own wedding ring. It will tell everyone: I am married to her. No one will ever replace my mother in my life.

The *People* reporter and photographer accompany me on the plane. All too soon we begin our descent to the Minneapolis airport. The photographer clicks off pictures while the reporter holds out a microphone and asks, "How do you feel?"

It's a good question, but I don't have a good answer. I am on overload, emotionless, numb.

The reporter and photographer leave the plane before me in order to capture the first instant of the reunion on film. I wait until everyone else has departed, then hoist Tiff into my arms and walk out the jetway. As I enter the airport, I can see the *People* people and... no one else. My birth family is nowhere in sight.

The reporter later compares my face at that moment to a child coming downstairs at Christmas and finding out Santa Claus hasn't come.

30

Minutes tick by. "Something awful must have happened," I say. The reporter is more productive, paging my birth family by white courtesy phone.

It is simply a case of wrong flight numbers; my birth family is at the wrong gate. We agree to meet at baggage claim. I hear Sue, yelling, "There she is! Jean! Hey, Jean!" and I am swept up by this wave of brothers and sisters, trying to hug everyone at once. It is a moment of pure joy.

Then Mike steps forward. He has held back with his mother, and now he parts the group surrounding me, like Moses parting the Red Sea, and there she is, the woman who gave birth to me, the one I have wondered about and thought about since I was a small child. She is trying very hard not to cry. I have told her I am like my mother, like Betty, and I do not cry in front of strangers. We share a brief, awkward hug, and then I back away.

I am not shy about embracing people, but I pull away from my birth mother at one of the most emotional moments of both our lives. It feels so wrong to be in her arms. I force a smile. "It's great to finally meet you," I say, then I carry Tiff around to meet everyone else, my nieces and nephews, a brother-in-law, a sister-in-law.

I hug all my brothers and sisters again and then Mike shakes my hand. Something clicks between us. His grip feels like an oar handle in my hand. I look over at Bobby and it is like looking in a mirror. He has tears in his eyes and a lump catches in my throat. I feel very loved, very missed.

I glance over at Lenore, standing to the side. I feel very confused.

We head in a caravan to Sue's house where we sit cross-legged on the living room floor, comparing our identical small hands and feet. I pull my three-inch search binder out of my suitcase, and Lenore looks through it politely. I know she wants everyone to leave the room so we can be alone, so we can talk, just the two of us, but I don't want to be alone with her. I want to regress and throw a pillow at someone.

When Mike and Jim and Bobby and Sue's husband Kevin jump into the pool for a game of water volleyball, I leave Tiff in Cathy's arms, put on my suit and dash out the door, giving a jungle yell as I dive in. Charles videotapes the moment, catching Lenore on tape rushing to the water's edge, hovering anxiously while I swim the length of the pool underwater. "Oh my god, oh my god! Is she okay, is she all right?" There is panic in her voice, as if I'm a toddler who has fallen in.

"No, Mom," Charles teases. "She's brain dead."

I surface and grab the ball from Mike and serve it up. I know I shouldn't be in the pool. I know I should be spending time with Lenore, working to resolve the emotions swirling around us, but it's much more appealing to play volleyball with my brothers and ignore her sad eyes. I don't want this drama. I want... I have no idea what I want, so I attack Bobby and pull him under water and wrestle the ball from his arms. I want to play and have these feelings go away.

We dress up and head to an elegant restaurant to celebrate Lenore's birthday. Everyone insists that I sit beside her, so I do, but with my back slightly turned so I can laugh and joke with my brothers and sisters. I grab Charles and tickle him, and when the birthday cake arrives, Bobby and I engage in a food fight. I am about eleven years old right now. Logline for episode one: the Brady children try to figure out their new relationships. It all begins to make sense during the cake fight.

I hand Lenore the birthday present I have made for her: a photo album with thirty-three pictures, one from each year of my life. Lenore acts excited. "Oh Jean, how lovely!" But as she looks through it, I notice that whenever Mom is in a photograph, Lenore instantly flips to the next page.

Jim gets to his feet and lifts his wine glass. "I want to wish Mother a happy birthday, and I want to welcome our sister Jean to the family. We're all grateful that you never gave up your search for us." He grins. "Here's to Christmas at your house this year!"

There is a rousing chorus of "Here, here!" as glasses are emptied and I look around the table at these warm-hearted people who have welcomed me to become one of them. I am so proud to be counted as part of their tribe.

But am I really one of them? Am I a reflection of what I have found? Is all of this going to change me?

Since the third grade, I have believed if I could just meet my birth family, everything would become clear. But on this first day with my original family, I am more confused than ever. Who am I? Am I supposed to be someone different?

I hug everyone good night and retreat to a hotel. Holding Tiff in my arms, I fall asleep. For the first night in a week, I do not have any trouble sleeping. And I do not dream. I do not dream anything at all.

31

"Call me Mom." Lenore says this to be nice, to be friendly, and because having her lost daughter call her Lenore is too painful, too distant.

"My mom is dead," I feel like shouting. "No one is ever taking her place, especially not you." Of course, I don't say this. I say, "Thanks, but I really wouldn't be comfortable calling you that." I escape, going to see *A Fish Called Wanda* with my brothers. We arrive at the theater late, laughing as we race from the parking lot, hurdling chains and barriers, arriving at our seats, breathless, just as the credits roll.

The next day, Lenore pulls me aside. "I need to be alone with you."

"Gee, I promised Jim and Cheryl I'd go see their house and Mike's giving me a tour of little Italy and..."

She reaches for my hand. "There are things I've waited to talk to you about in person. I feel such joy at knowing you're alive, to be able to see you, but I've felt anger too, about silly things I know, the name change, the baptism. I want to get past these feelings and get a chance for you to know the real me."

Didn't I already tell her that Cecilia didn't work with Sacconaghi? That my dad took me to church every Sunday? That I was baptized on Easter, the year I turned twelve. I clench my teeth. "I don't know what to say. I wouldn't want to change anything. I feel I was lucky to have been raised by my mom and dad."

She releases my hand and I know I have hurt her. What does she want from me?

It is the eve of Tiff's first birthday, and his new aunts and uncles and cousins throw a party for him, singing, "Happy Birthday dear Kristoffer," and clapping when he blows out the candle on top his cupcake. Everyone is trying so hard, but I can tell my behavior toward Lenore is affecting each of them. Everyone is exhausted.

That night, I stay on the sofa bed in the basement of the house where my brothers and sisters were raised. I listen to the hushed sounds of my birth family in the kitchen above, talking softly so I can sleep.

I am awake for hours. Who would I have been if I had grown up in this house? What if Lenore *had* come back for me after she and Lou married? How different would I have been?

"Lou would have loved for us to raise you," Lenore says.

I think about the field across the street from my house on La Cañada Road where the wild mustard grows three feet high in the spring and where all the kids in the neighborhood, me included, built tunnels through the grass, our green mazes leading to secret forts. I want to go home. I want my mom.

The next morning, Sue and Lenore take me to the airport. Our goodbyes are restrained. I know Sue is disappointed, baffled. It all started off so high, but there is no joy in our stiff hugs. A question hangs above us in the Minneapolis terminal. "What happened?" I get on the plane before I have to answer. What happened? My mom died, and Lenore wants to take her place.

My discomfort stretches far beyond my new family members. "I think it's so wonderful you've found your mother!" people say to me back in Worcester.

I nod politely, then say, "It's really exciting having all these new brothers and sisters."

"What's your mother like?" friends ask.

"*Birth* mother," I say curtly. "She's not my mom." I give them a lecture on the difference.

People magazine comes out. Our reunion is the lead story, September 5, 1988, focusing on my search, on my past, and Lenore's past. The reporter writes about my mom and dad and Lafayette and rowing. I like that he has done this, but I cringe at the heading under the title of the article:

Jean Strauss always wondered who her real mother was, and last month, after years of searching, she found out.

I write the editor of *People*. I thank him for covering the story, but take exception with the heading. "I know who my real mother was. She died a year and a half ago and I can never replace her." The editor probably thinks I am slightly tetched. Everyone else does, too. He can just get in line.

"What's wrong?" people ask. "We thought you wanted this."

"She's your mother, too," someone says gently.

"No, she's not!" The notion of two mothers seems as sacrilegious to me as there being two gods. I make my brothers and sisters "mine" without in any way accepting their mother. It doesn't feel disloyal to love them. I can have a dozen siblings, but only one mother.

Mike flies to Massachusetts for a visit. We play football on the front lawn and hike to the top of Mount Monadnock and marvel at the autumn colors at our feet. I show him my racing shell and my photo albums and the trunk full of things I cherished as a child. I show him me.

Mike is six-foot-four-drop-dead-gorgeous with dark brown hair and eyes, and though we don't look alike, I feel such a strong kinship with him. He *is* my brother and there is an emptiness inside me when he flies home.

Jim and his wife Cheryl fill the gap when they come a week later, bringing the ingredients for an Italian feast in their suitcase. We stay up until four in the morning talking and singing songs. Cheryl is pregnant like me, our babies due at the same time and I love having this sister-in-law who I can talk to about anything, and this brother who seems to like me in spite of how I am treating his mother.

When Jim leaves a few days later and hugs me at the airport, saying, "I love you Sis," I just melt. I have a brother who loves me. He does not write things on his forehead with a laundry marker and he is a kind man, who works hard to support his family. I call him my brother, introduce him to people as my brother. And his mother is simply someone I ignore.

When she calls, I cringe with guilt at her hushed voice. "I just wanted to know if you were still alive," she says. There is pain there. I know I'm the one causing it, but I don't like her letting me know.

"Why doesn't she just leave me alone?" I say to Jon.

"This is traumatic for both of you," he advises. "Be patient."

I try to explain my discomfort to Liz over lunch, and my dearest of friends doesn't give me the sympathy I expect. "You know, you searched for her," says Liz. "You disrupted her life. I think you're being way too hard on her."

"You don't understand," I snap. "You've never gone through anything like this."

"Still," Liz says, always willing to tell it like it is. "I think you owe her something. You turned her life upside down."

I almost stand up and shove the table over, I am so angry. White hot rage is not an emotion I am used to, particularly where best friends are concerned. Fortunately, I do not jump up and act as if I am Robert DeNiro in a movie, kicking the table over and screaming obscenities. I say quietly, "Why don't we talk about something else."

"Okay," says Liz, but I can tell by the look in her eyes: I have become someone she doesn't recognize.

I know how she feels. I am afraid to look in the mirror, afraid I will see hair growing on my cheeks and arms. I have become an adoptee werewolf who should be locked in a closet on nights with full moons.

This is not what I expected at all.

`

32

On the fifteenth of February, Tiff receives a Valentine in the mail without a return address on the envelope. Since he is only a year and a half old, I open it for him. It is from Lenore.

I read him the front and the greeting inside, but I do not read the signature. I do not tell him it says, 'With love from Grandma Lenore.' "Race you to the kitchen for an ice cream," I say and the card is forgotten. He beats me to the fridge, and when Tiff isn't looking, I throw the Valentine into the trash.

Of course, Lenore probably doesn't know that the fifteenth of February is the second anniversary of my mom's death. The timing is unfortunate. But half a year has passed since our reunion and I am more determined than ever to have no relationship with the woman who gave birth to me. How dare she call herself his grandmother!

I carry Tiff in my arms to the hallway upstairs, and point to people in the photos on the wall. "That's my dad, your Grandpa. He was the quarterback of the football team at Santa Barbara High. Can you say that? Quarterback."

"Courterack."

"Good! And this is my mom. This is your Grandma."

My son's small hand touches the picture on the wall. "Granma."

"That's right. Grandma."

In April, I give birth to my second son, Jonathon. Looking into his eyes, I have the strange sensation that I have known him for a long time. He is an old soul.

When I held Tiff right after he was born, it was the first time I'd ever seen anyone I was related to. It was an awesome moment.

Twenty months later, I have met many people I am related to, and my newborn son Jonathon leads me somewhere else. As I look into his eyes, he beckons me to stand in Lenore's shoes.

How would I feel if I had to give him away? I know the answer instantly. I would die. A part of me would just die. Is this what Lenore felt? It is the first empathetic thought I have for Lenore in a long time. But I'm not able to evaporate the dark clouds in my soul. Could it be I'm angry with her for having given me up? Could it be I've always been angry with her?

All I know is, I cannot give her what she needs. I cannot be Cecilia. I am Jean and Betty is the only mom I want. She should be here to hold her grandsons, to send them Valentine cards signed 'with love from Grandma.'

A week after Jonathon is born, Jim's wife Cheryl gives birth to a son, Reed. Who would have ever thought I would have nieces and nephews, and that my sons would have cousins their age.

We fly out and stay with them for a few days before Christmas and it is totally chaotic and wonderful watching Tiff and Jonathon and Taylor and Collin and Reed in their red Dr. Dentons crawling all over each other. All of them have ear infections so I stay hidden at Jim's behind bottles of Ceclor and Tylenol.

"The kids are sick," I tell Lenore in a brief phone conversation. "I'll see you at Sue's party."

Sue and Kevin host a holiday celebration at their multi-level home, and I shift from room to room, laughing with my brothers and sisters, avoiding Lenore. Midway through the evening, Cheryl and Sue have a surprise for everyone. They have transferred all the Iacarella family home movies onto videotape with a music soundtrack. As I catch glimpses of my brothers and sisters growing up, I witness a life that might have been: Cecilia's.

It is time to go. I fetch the baby bag from Sue's bedroom on the top floor, and with Tiff holding my hand, walk toward the stairs only to find Lenore standing on the catwalk in front of me. I am trapped.

"We need to talk," she says.

I back away. "We were just leaving. The kids are still on antibiotics and I really should get them to bed."

Tiff is looking through the rails, down at the first floor.

"I never know what to say to you," Lenore says. "I'm always afraid anything I say just makes you more angry."

"Angry?" I smile, civilly. "I'm not angry."

"You have to understand, I had no choice."

Tiff inspects a plant hanging on the wall just beyond his reach.

"You did have a choice," I say, my voice not so civil.

There are tears forming in her eyes. "No. I didn't."

Tiff's small hand stretches out through the railing.

"Yes you did," I say. "You chose between your parents and me, society and me, the church and me. And it was the right choice!"

Lenore sobs. "No it wasn't!"

Suddenly there is a loud "Smash!" as Tiff unhooks the hanging plant and it falls twelve feet, shattering on the floor below us, dirt and roots everywhere on the white rug. I scoop Tiff into my arms. What a brilliant child, an enchanting child. "I better go clean that up," I say, sliding past Lenore, leaving her alone on the catwalk. I do not know if she is crying. I do not look back.

She writes me a letter that night. "Dear Jean... I don't think we should ever see each other again. It is too hard and hurts too much... I want to remember Cecilia the way she was... I wish you well..." The letter sits on her desk for a week, then she tears it up, telling me about it much later.

On a trip to California, I take Mike to the house where I grew up on La Cañada Road. The owner graciously lets us wander from room to room. "This is the hallway where I learned to walk, and this was Frankie's room, and my room, and this was my dad's barbeque pit." We walk down the path to the backyard. "This was the hothouse where my grandfather grew his prize orchids. And there's the garden where I kept my horse." I bring my brother home, connecting him to my past.

We hike to the creek where I used to play. Even though Mike and I are in our thirties, we slide down the sandy slope like a couple of kids, exploring the thickets, floating sticks in the water, and skipping stones. I chuck a heavy rock into the creek, splashing Mike, dashing up the hill ahead of him. We might not have grown up together, but we are brother and sister now.

While staying at a cabin in the wine country we drive together to visit a neighbor and en route talk about the awkward relationship I have with Lenore. "It seems to me," I say, "that being a family isn't about being related as much as it's about sharing experiences with each other."

"Makes sense," says Mike as we pull up the dirt driveway to the rustic A-frame where a sign in the window warns us, 'Forget about the dog - beware of the owner.' The front door opens, and our reclusive neighbor steps out holding onto the collar of his enormous Great Dane.

I hop out of the car. I have met both the man and the dog before, and reach out my hand to them both. "Hi boy," I say to the dog. The Dane lunges from his owner's grip and sinks his teeth through my right hand. I feel the bones crunch as I sink to the ground.

"Jean!" Mike rushes to my side as the man yanks back his dog. The neighbor pulls me into his kitchen and shoves my hand under the sink faucet, turning on the cold water. Mike stands behind me. "You all right?"

I feel ready to pass out. "I don't know."

"You're fine," the neighbor says hopefully. "It's just a scratch."

I look down and see chunks of flesh hanging out a hole through my hand. Mike steps forward. "You don't look so good." He puts his arm around me. "Come on. I'm taking you to the hospital."

The nearest emergency room is half hour away. I feel queasy and lightheaded and glad Mike is talking nonstop. When a doctor pokes a syringe into the wound through my hand, I look away, up at Mike. "What're you grinning at?"

"I was just thinking," he says. "You were right, what you said earlier. It's experiences like this that will make us a family." I laugh then. And I am not surprised at all when it turns out Mike is absolutely right.

33

"I'm afraid of flying," Lenore says.

"Not me," I lie. "I learned to fly when I was in college."

Actually, this is true. Annie, a member of the varsity crew at Cal, had just earned her instructor's certificate and I was her very first student. "I want to learn," I told her, "so I won't be afraid when I travel." Whenever I had enough money to rent a plane, she would take me up. She was a great teacher, and I enjoyed the mechanics of flying, the coordination of the ailerons and rudder and flaps. The day finally arrived when I soloed.

"Don't crash," Annie joked. "It'll look bad on my resume if I lose my first student."

I didn't crash. I survived my first solo, and my second and third, and then did a longer cross-country flight. But, as I approached the final test for my pilot's license, I ran out of money and Annie went home for summer vacation. Four months passed before Annie and I drove back to the Hayward Airport and rented a plane.

We took off, me in the pilot seat, her in the co-pilot's, and did some practice landings and take-offs. "You're doing great!" she said. "You haven't forgotten a thing. Why don't you do three touch-and-goes on your own and then we'll fly out to Livermore."

I was feeling very confident. I took off alone and circled the airport, gently guiding the white two-seater Cessna down for a landing. It was a beauty, smooth and controlled, the best landing I had ever done, and I could see Annie cheering me on the grass strip at the edge of the runway as I rolled past and accelerated for my second take-off. The instant I eased back on the wheel and the plane left the ground, a question popped into my mind, a really stupid question. "What would happen if I passed out up here?" My heart did a sis-boom-bah and my brain spat out an answer. "You'll crash! You're gonna die!" All of a sudden, everything got very bright. My hands sweaty, my heart racing, I felt very disoriented. I knew what was happening, I'd hyperventilated before, but never when I was alone, eight hundred feet in the air. I called the tower to inform them. "I'm really scared up here."

"Yeah?" The gum-chewing controller was unimpressed. "You're cleared for the pattern."

"You don't understand! I'm hyperventilating! What should I do?"

There was a long gum-snapping pause before he said, "Try singing."

Singing?

"It's a long way, to Tipperary, a long way to go." I don't know why this song popped into my head, but I think it had something to do with Snoopy and the Red Baron. I gripped the wheel tightly, my knuckles white, as I tried to remember the words while I flew parallel to the runway on the downwind leg. I turned onto final, sweat pouring down my face. "It's a long way, to Tipperary, so smile boys that's the show!" I belted out lyrics to a song I didn't really know as I lined up the little Cessna with the runway. My angle was too steep and the plane hit the tarmac hard and bounced, like a rabbit with wings, hopping down the runway until I could slow down enough that the wheels stayed on the ground and I braked to a stop near Annie.

She ran up to the plane and cracked open the door. "What happened?" she shouted over the noise of the engine.

"I don't know."

"Well, let's go right back up."

"No." I knew. "I'm done Annie."

"What?"

"I'm about ready to get a license that will allow me to carry other people. What am I going to do if I hyperventilate with passengers on board? Ask them to take over?"

"I hyperventilate," my birth mother tells me.

"Really? What's that?" I refuse to acknowledge any similarity between us.

"I'm afraid of flying," she admits.

"Not me," I lie. "I love to fly."

Jon holds my hand as the DC-10 rolls down the runway. We are on our way to Bermuda to celebrate our tenth wedding anniversary and when the plane levels off at thirty-five thousand feet, the fuselage twists and the walls rattle. Flight attendants come down the aisle with their hands gently touching the overhead bins, as if this gesture will save them from smashing their heads against the ceiling when we hit an air pocket. Usually flight attendants smile at passengers so we will not panic, so we will believe everything is fine, but they are not smiling today. I sit with my seat belt tightly buckled wondering if they know something we don't know.

Jon doesn't share my concern. On his lap is a book, How We Die. I feel this is an odd choice of reading material for an airplane flight, much less a romantic holiday, but he is not reading, instead he's sound asleep, his head tilted back, a slight smile on his lips. I resent him for this.

"I'm a worrier," admits Lenore.

"Not me," I say. "Worrying accomplishes nothing."

I don't tell her that before Jon and I leave for Bermuda, I type an entire manual of instructions in the event something should happen to us on the trip. I send these pages to the people we have chosen as the boys' guardians, as well as our executor. In addition, I update my will, last minute directions describing how the world should continue should I perish, as if I will be able to control events and circumstances after my demise, something I have not mastered while alive. But I do not admit any of this to Lenore. Instead I tell her, "I never worry about anything."

Jon awakens just as the plane touches the ground. He leans over, prying my hands from the armrests. "Good flight?"

Oh yeah. "What I want to know," I say in the taxi on the way to the hotel, "is why they can't make the whole plane out of the stuff they use in those black boxes."

"The plane would never get off the ground."

"Oh."

We rent two little red mopeds and zip along the two lane highways of Bermuda on the left side of the road. I race past Jon, the wind bringing tears to my eyes. He shakes his head when he pulls alongside me at a stop sign. "You're nervous about flying in a jet, but you'll go fifty miles an hour on a moped?"

"I'm wearing a helmet."

"It's not made out of the material the black boxes are."

I laugh, pulling out ahead of him, my long skirt flying behind me. "Race you to the hotel!" I shout over my shoulder.

"I tend to focus on worst case scenarios," Lenore confesses.

"Not me," I say, even though before I leave for Bermuda, I worry about some mild chest pain I am experiencing, convinced it is some form of fatal heart disease. My doctor does some tests. "I think you're just under stress," she says. "You shouldn't worry."

"You mean there's nothing wrong or you mean I should worry about my worrying?"

The doctor presses her lips together, suppressing a smile. "Both."

I do not tell Lenore about this. I do not tell her that we have things in common. I tell her I am strong, I am powerful, I am like my mom, I am like Betty.

This is what I want Lenore to see. When she looks at me, I don't want her to think of me as any kind of a mirror. I want her to see a reflection of Betty. I want her to know: I am just like my mom.

34

What does Lenore want from me? Who would I have been if she had raised me instead of Mom? Will everyone forget that Betty is my real mother?

I am asking the wrong questions.

I have known my birth mother almost two years, yet I continue to remain stuck in first gear, unable to move forward. When I learn about a man on Long Island who helps members of the adoption triad work through the reunion process, I am hopeful he'll be able to help me. Perhaps this is a sign I am ready for a relationship with Lenore: I don't want to feel angry anymore.

This long-reunited adoptee and I talk. His approach is to get me to focus on goals. What do I want to have happen? What's realistic to target? He asks me a simple question. "What would Lenore have to do for you to be comfortable with her?"

It is a good question. I have no response, but a few hours later, the answer flashes in my mind like a neon sign. What would Lenore have to do? Simple. Accept that Betty was, and will always be, my mom. If Lenore could accept that fact, it would mean she accepted me and my adoptive family and the reality of who I am. We could become friends. For the first time since we first met, something inside me relaxes. I want to be friends.

But what can I do to help Lenore accept my mom? Sue and Cheryl's Christmas home movie video gives me an idea. I transfer my parents' home movies to video tape and create a mini-documentary, mailing off a copy to Lenore. I'm surprised how anxious I am to hear her reaction.

She calls immediately after receiving it. "Your tape was terrific!" she says. "For the first time, I feel like I did the right thing. I can see that your parents loved you so much."

Your parents. Her saying this lifts a barrier inside me. It is a beginning.

Two years to the day after we first met, I fly to Minnesota to see my birth family. It is not just a social visit. Sue organizes a therapy session with a pair of psychologists for the whole family to discuss what has been happening since my arrival. I'm terrified. I know I've caused a strain within the family, that I've disappointed and confused everyone. I feel I am about to enter the lions den.

But as the ten of us talk around the table, I realize that the reunion has been the catalyst for individual growth in each of us. I find myself jumping to Lenore's defense more than once. "No one can understand what she's been through," I say. "The year and a half she spent in an orphanage, her own adoption, her relinquishment of me. These events affected other choices she has made."

After the session is over, Lenore and I surprise everyone by going out to lunch together. We have never done anything alone, just the two of us, before. We sit in Marie Callander's and reach across the table with words.

"I wish I could have met Betty," Lenore says.

"And I wish she could have met you. She would have helped us make sense of all of this."

We talk about the book I am writing about searches and reunions. "May I read it?" Lenore asks. "I've decided I want to search for my own birth mother."

"What information do you have?"

Lenore reveals she has a powerful clue from her past. "I have my original birth certificate."

I almost do a cartwheel right there in front of the salad bar. I take my paper Marie Callender placemat and begin to make notes. "What was your given name at birth?"

"Lenora Cecilia Brown."

I flash on a name from my distant past: Elam *Brown* was the founder of Lafayette, my home town. I wonder if we are related as I write down Lenore's name. "Okay, and what was your birth mother's name?"

"Mary Teresa Brown."

Mary Brown? Could she have had a more common name? "Okay."

"She was born in Wisconsin, but gave birth to me in Oregon."

"And how old was she then?"

"Twenty."

1934 minus twenty. "Okay, so she was born in 1914 or 1915."

"I suppose so, yes."

"This," I smile, "is going to be a snap."

I have been known to be wrong on occasion. This is one of those times.

35

As my birth mother and I embark on a search for Mary Teresa Brown, we also begin a tentative friendship. But there are still cold war borders between us, boundaries that I make clear are not to be crossed. I call frequently to give her advice on ways in which she can try to find Mary, but I never call for motherly advice. I have not swung wide the door, but merely cracked it open.

However, I have invited other women to become my mentors, to mother me through motherhood. They all share the same qualification: they were friends of my mom's. When I hear their voices, I also hear hers.

The day Mom learned she was going to die, she'd made a joke, saying, "Well, I wouldn't have been a whole lot of help to you anyway since I never gave birth."

I hadn't laughed. I'd said, "I don't think giving birth has anything to do with being a good mother." And I was right. All those breathing exercises hadn't helped at all on the day I brought Tiff home from the hospital and tried to give him a bath in one of those little plastic bathtubs.

I put in the plug, filled the tub with warm water, set it on the changing table, and gently placed my tiny son into it. Immediately he started peeing, water spraying everywhere, as if from an uncontrolled hose. I couldn't do anything without submerging him, so I stood there laughing and Tiff kicked his feet and uncorked the plug and warm bath water joined the pee and ran all over the changing table and down onto all of his neatly stacked diapers and clothes.

I put the plastic bathtub on a high shelf in the garage and used the sink after that. I advise Tiff: I am learning to be a parent with you. You're a passenger in a plane with an inexperienced pilot. Please keep your seatbelt tightly fastened at all times.

On Christmas Eve, a dusting of snow covers the ground and Jon builds a roaring fire in the fireplace. I put five-month-old Tiff on a mattress on the floor where he does pushups in the light of the dancing flames. I smile, watching him, not knowing he is about to have a major breakthrough in life: he's about to roll over for the first time.

I witness the event. Tiff does a beautiful little Eskimo roll right off the mattress and onto the floor, a hideous "Thud!" following as his head bangs on the hard wood. He cries out in pain and I rush to lift him into my arms. What should I do? My mother is gone, there are no tribal elders next door I can consult, so I race into the kitchen and call his doctor. "My son's just fallen!" I shout to the receptionist who answers the phone. "He's hit his head and he's only five months old. Should I take him to the emergency room?"

The pediatrician on call rings me right back and I explain it all again. "Okay," she says calmly. "Slow down. Is he conscious?"

"Yes."

"Are his eyes dilated?"

"I don't think so."

"Is he vomiting?"

"No."

"And how far did he fall?"

I peer at the mattress, trying to gauge the height exactly. "Five inches, maybe six."

It sounds like a stifled laugh on the other end of the phone, but perhaps the doctor is just clearing her throat. "This is your first child, isn't it Mrs. Strauss?"

"Yes. What should I do?"

"I'd recommend a nice glass of wine in front of the fire. He's just fine. And you will be too in a few minutes."

Slowly, I begin to learn about motherhood. My growth as a parent becomes evident two years later, when Jonathon is five months old, sitting in his carrier on the kitchen table, and Tiff accidentally knocks over a chair, which bangs into the carrier and my five-month-old baby is catapulted into the air, landing face down on the linoleum floor where he cries out in pain. I lift him into my arms, hold him close, examining his face, his eyes, and I relax. "It's okay, you'll be okay," I murmur as I carry him past the phone to the rocking chair in the living room.

That's the difference between one's first child and one's second.

I do not call Lenore for advice when such things happen, but I do call my other mothers: Mom's friend, Lue; Linda's mom, Jackie; my Aunt Marty and Aunt Rena. They guide me through each crisis.

"Jonathon's getting four teeth all at once and he's crying a lot. What should I do?"

"Put Grand Marnier on his gums."

"Tiff's barking like a seal."

"That's croup. Take him into the bathroom and turn the hot water on in the shower and stay there with him in the steam for twenty minutes."

I hear giggling in the kitchen as I fold clothes in the dining room and smile at the happy sounds of my sons playing some game they've invented. When I go to check on them, however, I discover that Tiff has poured an entire canister of orange Metamucil over Jonathon's head. Two-year-old Jonathon, quite honored by Tiff's gesture, is proudly licking Metamucil off his arms, his shirt, the floor. I call my other mothers.

"Is Metamucil dangerous?"

"Check with poison control," they advise, "and then buy some extra diapers."

Sometimes, it is my sons who guide me. One afternoon, Jonathon has his new pre-school friend Gabriel over to play, and the two four-year-olds race off together, pretending they are Power Rangers.

Two hours later, when Gabriel's mom is due to pick him up, Jonathon peeks his head around the laundry room door. "Hey Mom! Come see what

Tiff and I did!" He leads me by the hand to the living room. Everything is fine, except that Gabriel's beautiful blond hair is a deep forest green.

"It works," says Tiff, proudly holding up the bottle of green dye that came with his chemistry set.

I don't know Gabriel's mom at all, outside of setting up this play date, and I'm not sure how she'll feel about her son coming home with a new hair color. We race to the kitchen sink and I try to wash the dye out with water. This only makes it worse. Not only is Gabriel's hair still green, but his face and neck are now green, too.

I can't reach my other mothers, but Jonathon keeps his head. "Here Mom," he says, handing me a bottle. "Try soap."

It works, sort of. At least Gabriel's hair isn't as shocking a green when his mother arrives. She is very nice about the situation. "Perhaps Jonathon can play at our house next time."

That night at bedtime, when Gabriel's father asks him if he was upset when Tiff and Jonathon dyed his hair green, Gabriel nods vigorously. "I wanted it to be orange."

I do not call Lenore for advice about Metamucil or croup or how to remove green dye from blond hair because I do not want to invite her to take Mom's place. But I do call her. We are becoming friends.

When she moves back to Minnesota, I come for a visit with the boys. She has married Don, the man she was dating, and they have bought a home not far from Jim's house. Lenore is outside retrieving her mail and I stand in her new living room, surrounded by moving boxes, Jonathon asleep in my arms. Suddenly, Tiff says, "Look Mommy! It's Grandma."

I spin around, the familiar knee jerk reaction in my gut. Lenore isn't Grandma. Betty is Grandma!

Sure enough, there's Lenore outside the window, walking up the front steps. But Tiff is not looking at her. He is seated on the floor beside a cardboard box, an open photo album on his lap: the album I gave Lenore the first day I met her. He is pointing at a picture of my mom, at Betty. "See," he says. "Grandma."

My voice catches and I can barely say, "That's right Tiff, that's her."

It's the moment I realize: I do not have to hold Lenore at bay to protect my mother's memory. My mom will be a part of our lives as long as we remember her.

36

Today, I am meeting my birth father. He does not want to meet me. He does not believe he is my father. He does not want to believe it.

I wrote him a week after I found Lenore.

> *It is difficult to know how to begin a letter like this... Five years ago, I began to search for my natural "roots". I was simply curious about my genetic past and interested in my medical background... Last week I found (my birth mother). I asked who you were and she told me. She was not even sure if you were still alive... Please don't be alarmed. I have no intention of interfering in your life...*

He never wrote back. I waited a year, then wrote him again. I didn't badger him, I nudged. I understood how unsettling something like this could be, but at the same time, I was perplexed. How could he not be curious about a child he fathered?

I finally spoke to him on the phone. He was polite, but cold, and in his voice I sensed both neutrality and fear. I waited yet another year and wrote him again. I never contacted him at home, always at work, and never identified myself to anyone but him. Still, he was threatened by any contact.

Three years after my first letter, while accompanying Jon on a business trip to the region of the country where my birth father lives, I contact him one last time. I tell him it would mean a great deal for me to meet him, that I believe it will put my curiosity to rest. "If accidental paternity carries any responsibility," I say, "it's a half hour over a cup of coffee." I almost gasp when he agrees, suggesting a restaurant where we can meet.

I arrive early to find the restaurant closed, the parking lot deserted. Standing alone on the black asphalt, I wonder why would he tell me to come to a restaurant that's closed? He wouldn't agree to meet me then stand me up and abandon me all over again, would he?

I don't even know what kind of car he drives. Why didn't I ask him that? Every car that comes down the road past the restaurant brings me to my feet. A Volvo. A Chevy. A pickup truck. A Ford. No one slows down, no one stops. Why would they? The restaurant is closed. This must be a joke. Ha, ha.

Would it help if he knew that I'm apprehensive, that I'm just like him, afraid of the unknown. Paranoia sets in. I vacillate between feeling sure he won't come, and feeling sure if he does, he'll try to mow me down with his car in this deserted parking lot. I envision the headlines. "Unknown Woman Found Splattered Across the Pavement At Sid's Diner. There Were No Witnesses." I'll look like Wiley Coyote flattened by a steam roller.

I stare at the road, the cars whizzing past. It's nine o'clock on the nose. And wait - there is a car turning into the lot, right on time. It parks near me and a man gets out, a man dressed in a forest green sports coat and a shirt and tie that don't quite match.

This is my birth father. There is a statement in his choice of clothes: take me as I am. "Hi."

"Hello." He is six feet tall, two hundred pounds, just like the description, only now I have a face to go with it.

"The restaurant's not open," I say.

"Yes, I can see that." He does not look me in the eye. "There's another coffee shop a mile from here. Why don't you follow me in your car."

"Okay."

There is no hug, nor even a handshake. This is not a joyful reunion, this is an obligation. I follow his car down the highway to another restaurant and we walk apart from each other to the door.

"It's always been my experience that reality doesn't measure up to fantasy," he says, holding the door open.

"Reality is what this is all about," I say, stepping inside.

We are shown to a booth and order coffee. "You want menus?" asks the waitress.

"No," says my birth father. "Just coffee." We're on a tight schedule here, a half hour and nothing more.

"I appreciate you doing this," I say.

"My wife doesn't know about you."

Fear is with us in this booth.

"As far as I'm concerned," I say, "she doesn't have to." I can see he doesn't understand why I needed to see him. I can feel him asking, "Why not leave well enough alone?"

I've thought about what I have a right to ask. His personal life is off limits. All I want is a past, a family tree. "I've always felt my parents are my parents," I say, "but I never felt their ancestors are my ancestors. Do you know anything about your family history?"

He pauses, looking at his coffee, as if reading tea leaves. "I've never understood this fascination some people have with genealogy."

I want to tell him it begins in the third grade. It is inspired by a blank page.

"I don't really know much about my family. My mother had English origins. Her family migrated from the Northeast to the Midwest. My father was also of English descent." He tells me his father's occupation, his grandfather's.

It's not much, but it makes me excited. My ancestors were immigrants! Well, aren't everyone's? Yes, but these are mine! I envision them traveling from the Northeast to the Midwest. How inspiring! This is the first ancestral history I have ever known and it thrills me to the core, even in its stripped down, no names, no anecdotes, version. I have a family tree, it just doesn't have any names on it.

My birth father has grown children, so I have more half brothers and sisters. I never learn their names. I do not ask. It doesn't feel right to ask. But he tells me a little bit about them, their ages, and what they've studied in college.

I say, "They sound like great people."

"Well, yes they are, though they've all done things that have gone against the grain of my own moral upbringing."

I am astounded, and ask the only prying question of the day. "Like what?"

"Living with their boyfriends and girlfriends before they got married. Things like that."

I nod. Now I understand. Falling from such a high pedestal would be a scary proposition. For him to acknowledge me would cost too much. I know I'll never meet these other siblings. And I can accept why.

He has always questioned his paternity and brings up the issue now. "I don't want to impugn your birth mother, but there is a possibility that I am not your birth father."

A possibility. This means he knows there is a possibility that he is.

"I believe Lenore," I say. "She's an adoptee herself and understands better than anyone my need to know the truth."

We talk about his career. The town he lives in. The goddamn weather.

"More coffee?" asks the waitress.

He holds up his hand. The half-hour glass is draining of sand. My time with my birth father is almost up.

We walk to the parking lot in silence. I ask if I can take his picture, and I'm grateful when he says, "Yes." A picture lasts forever. But this reunion will not.

"Thanks," I say, holding out my hand. He reaches out to hug me instead. It takes me by surprise, and though it lasts just a moment, it is a good hug. As I feel his arms around me, I know this is not only the first time, but the only time.

I hug him back. Hard.

37

"Your book is helping me so much." Lenore's words make me very glad I have written about the experiences of those involved in search and reunion. But I quickly learn I have stuck my hand in the flame of rejection by publishing a book.

I travel to New Orleans, for a national adoption conference, where the book is to be officially launched. These are my people, these members of the adoption triad, and I should feel safest with them, but I don't. Even before I reach the conference, a triad member sends a vitriolic letter to my publisher, attacking my credentials. Another shuns me completely in New Orleans, making for an uncomfortable launching rather than a joyful one. I learn that when one writes a book about something so personal and complex, others who have gone through the same experience, but with different perspectives, can feel mis-portrayed, if not betrayed.

I come to the lobby of the hotel to meet Jerry and Maria, two birth parents I interviewed for Birthright. We have never met face-to-face, and by chance, they are in New Orleans, saw the sign for the adoption conference, and stop by the hotel simply to see if I am in attendance. They have a plane to catch, so we have only a few minutes. It is a brief but emotional moment as we embrace. "How's everything going with you?" I ask, knowing the pain they have been through during their reunion with their birth daughter.

"Better," they say, and it is good to see them hopeful, smiling. "What are you up to now?"

I tell them about a children's book I have written, an adoption tale about a cheetah raised by a pride of lions, about the young cheetah's struggle to fit in and how she learns the only way to belong is to be herself. "It sounds wonderful," they say, hugging me quickly as they dash off to catch their plane.

Only then do I glance around the lobby and realize that many of the conference participants are amassing. Everyone is going to an off site event and I am not invited. "I didn't tell you," a friend says gently. "I didn't want to hurt your feelings." Waves of rejection crash over me. I stand off to the side, fighting the urge to cry, as everyone gets into taxis and depart without me.

I decide to do something proactive. The story I have written about the cheetah cuts to the heart of how I see adoption, how I see myself. I have tried, in vain, to find a cheetah pendant back home, but I am in the antique center of New Orleans. I am sure I will find one here. So I venture into the streets of New Orleans, my cheetah quest occupying my thoughts, holding my feelings of abandonment at bay.

I go to one shop, then another, block after block, store after store. Nothing. I walk all the way down to the Mississippi River, to the huge mall on the waterfront. Not one single cheetah.

Then I realize: the zoo. Of course. The New Orleans Zoological Park! They're sure to have a cheetah pin, a cheetah pendant, a cheetah something. The streetcar named Desire drops me off a mile from the zoo, and I make the hike in the hot sun, confident I will find a cheetah.

There are seven stores at the zoo. Seven. But not one of them has a cheetah. There are leopards and lions and tigers and panthers, every kind of wild cat imaginable, except cheetahs. As I make my way back to the hotel, I am overcome by a sense of failure. I have walked ten miles, yet I am returning empty handed. I open the door to my dark hotel room and flip on the light, flop on the bed, then glance over at the telephone. The little red message light is blinking. The hotel operator informs me, "There's an envelope for you at the front desk."

An envelope? It must be a note from the person I'm supposed to have dinner with, saying something like, "Sorry kid, I've got a much better offer. Besides, you're such a loser. I don't think I should be seen with you."

The receptionist at the front desk hands me a hotel envelope, thick and lumpy in my hand. What on earth is this? I open the envelope and almost fall over.

Inside is a cheetah hanging on a necklace cord.

Accompanying it is a note from Jerry and Maria, the birth parents I interviewed by phone, who I never met in person until today. They had asked me what I was working on now, and I had told them about the story of the cheetah adopted by a lion pride. I hadn't told them I was going to spend the day looking for one. They'd been leaving to catch a plane. How had they found a cheetah in a city with no cheetahs?

It has been here all day, this cheetah, waiting for me while I walked the streets of New Orleans. These strangers, who are not really strangers at all, transform me. Today, they are my family.

The world can be dark and unkind, but these birth parents have provided me with food for my soul, a sheltering sense of belonging. I clutch the cheetah tightly in my hand and race for the elevator before I start bawling right there in the middle of the lobby.

38

"These records are sealed. You have no right to this information." Lenore is sixty years old and I am astounded people say such a thing to her when she asks for their help, but she is told this frequently. "You cannot see these documents which contain information about you."

"This is harder than I thought," Lenore says, when door after door is closed in her face.

"Don't worry," I say. "We know your birth mother's name. This isn't going to take long." But I am wrong. It is not a snap like I told Lenore it would be in Marie Callander's. The search for Mary Teresa Brown drags on and on, month after month.

When I first saw Lenore's original birth certificate, I saw many things we could do to locate Mary. She was born in Fond du Lac, Wisconsin. There should be a record of her birth, but there is not. In 1934, she was living in a small town in Oregon. There should be some record of her there, at schools, in old phone books, something, but there is nothing. Mary Teresa Brown is invisible. A year passes, then another and another, and I begin to wonder if she ever existed at all.

"Where is she?" Lenore asks. "She couldn't just disappear." But she has. I reach out to Lenore as she faces the slammed doors, the dead ends. More than anyone in the family, I understand what she is going through. We talk almost daily and her search becomes our bond.

Her husband Don is a pillar of support, making journeys with her to Wisconsin, spending hours reading microfilm records, visiting Catholic churches, cemeteries, high schools. When their efforts yield nothing, he keeps her spirits up. "Don't worry. We'll find her."

He accompanies Lenore to Oregon, and the two of them repeat the process: the county records, the libraries, the schools and cemeteries, and again they are unable to find any information. Documents do exist that would help them, but they are not allowed to see these. At the Catholic Archdiocese in Portland, when a clerk turns Lenore away, Don presses. "Please, there must be something."

"When I say there's nothing," says the clerk, "I mean nothing."

"No," Don snaps, "you mean you won't help a sixty-year-old woman find her family."

They drive to Catholic Family Services next, and tell the director they must find Lenore's birth mother before time runs out. Every month that passes decreases the chance they will find her alive. The director says, "The records are sealed. I can't let you see them."

"Are you married?" Don asks.

"Yes."

"Well how would you feel if your spouse needed this information, and people with access to it denied her the right to see it?"

The man shrugs. "I have to follow the rules. I'm sorry."

"Don't be discouraged," Don says to Lenore on the flight home. "We're never giving up."

Two years later, they return to Oregon again, this time driving to the little town outside Portland that is listed on the birth certificate as Lenore's birth father's residence. His name was Georg, and they hunt for him in high school yearbooks and local records and cemeteries, all to no avail. With nothing left to do, they literally stop people on the village streets.

"Excuse me, did you live here during the nineteen thirties?"

One man they stop is involved in the local historical society, and he knows of an elderly woman who lived in the area during the Depression. They call her, and she invites Lenore and Don into her home. The old woman reaches out and takes my birth mother's hand. "I knew Georg."

"What?"

"I did. He worked on my dad's berry ranch. He played the violin."

Tears fall upon Lenore's cheeks. Her father played the violin! Music is her life. She has performed it and taught it all her days. Now she knows where the gift came from. The woman continues. "He had a German accent. He and his mother emigrated here after World War One. The transition was hard for them. They'd been in the middle class, but here they were just considered poor immigrants."

"Where is he now?" Lenore asks. "My father, Georg, where?"

"The last time I saw him was over fifty years ago, when they moved to the big city, to Portland." She smiles. "Georgie was his mother's whole life."

Lenore and Don find other people in the area who also knew her birth father. "I went to high school with Georg," says an elderly man. "He was a very pleasant fellow. Couldn't speak English well, but boy could he play the violin."

Lenore shakes the man's wrinkled hand. She is touching people that knew her birth father. "Where is he now?"

"I'm sorry," says the old man. "It's been so long, I just don't know."

One woman was friends with Mia, Georg's mother. "What was she like?" Lenore asks.

"Forceful," says the woman. "I liked her, but she could be intimidating. She ran a little business on the fourth floor of a building in downtown Portland, and worked very hard."

"What happened to her? To her son?"

"It's been decades since I saw either of them."

"Do you have any pictures of them?"

The old woman looks up at the ceiling, speaking slowly. "I don't have pictures, but I can tell you that Georg had brown eyes and hair and a wide face. A nice face." For the first time in her life, Lenore has an image of her father in her mind. She knows the color of his hair.

Then a miracle happens. Don and Lenore drive to the orphanage where Lenore was adopted. There, a sympathetic clerk hands Lenore an index card with all the information she has been seeking.

Mary Frances Brown. Age 18.
Religion: Roman Catholic.
Born: Fond du Lac, Wisconsin 8/21/1915
High School: Madeleine. Graduated.
Mother: not living.
Father: Living. A carpenter
Child born: Lenora Cecilia Brown 8/10/1934
Father: Georg (first admitted, then denied)
Grandfather: Edwin A. Brown II
Grandmother: Flora/died/1927 Oregon T.B. Hospital

Lenore calls. "I've found them!" As she tells me everything she's learned, I'm stunned. We know names. Mary *Frances* Brown. We know places. Addresses. She's done it. Lenore has done it!

But the euphoria soon ebbs as these new clues lead only to more dead ends. Lenore can find no records for Mary Frances Brown, no trace of her, anywhere. She has met people who knew her birth father, she knows more about both Mary and Georg than ever before, but she has not found *them*. Mary and Georg have disappeared from the face of the earth.

I don't know how to say these words to Lenore. "We've tried everything. For six years, you have done your best. But it's over. We're never going to find them."

I say nothing. Making her face this harsh reality serves no real purpose. The mere act of searching for her birth family has strengthened Lenore so much, and united us in a way that nothing else, not even our blood ties, has ever done. Why impose a conclusion on such a positive process?

But even though I say nothing, I know the truth: the search for Mary Frances Brown is over.

39

Mid-September, Jon and I take the boys to Harper's Ferry for a weekend outing on a gray afternoon. We walk from one exhibit to the next, tracing the activities of the infamous John Brown, the abolitionist who terrorized this town in 1859, and ended up being hanged for his deeds. As we stroll up the main street, window-shopping, eight-year-old Tiff runs ahead of us and disappears into an antique photo store, one of those places full of cowboy and gambler costumes, and we follow him inside.

Tiff turns to us. "Can I have my picture taken?"

Jon and I share a surprised glance. Tiff *hates* having his picture taken. Since the time he was barely a year old, a camera pointed his direction always evokes a scowl. "No. It costs twenty dollars." Tiff leaves without complaint, but later, when we pass the shop on our way down the hill, he makes his appeal again, and this time we say, "Okay."

Carefully and meticulously, without seeking any advice from us, Tiff chooses his costume from the racks and disappears into the dressing room. I assume he will be a gunslinger, as his older cousins had done in a photo he'd seen, but when Tiff reappears, he is a small and very serious Union Army soldier.

Avoiding us, he steps in front of the camera. "I need a sword and a pistol," he instructs the photographer. She brings these, along with a drum. "But," he protests, "I'm not a drummer boy." She nods, but leaves the drum where it is. The light flashes, the aperture clicks, and a moment is frozen in time.

The resultant photograph is hauntingly similar to pictures I have seen of soldiers during the Civil War. Tiff stares straight at the lens, a young man ready to do his duty, the pistol in his hand, the sword resting on his shoulder. He seems much older than his eight years. It's such a striking photograph that we buy a large, framed copy which we later hang in the upstairs hallway.

At the park entrance, buoyed by Tiff's heretofore never-displayed interest in being photographed, I pull out my camera and say, "Let me get a picture of the three of you."

It is as if the events minutes earlier in the photo shop never occurred. Tiff's face darkens. "Mom. You know I hate having my picture taken." Jon looks at me and we both shrug.

Two months pass. In mid-November, Lenore leaves a message on the answering machine. "Jean! I can't believe you're not home. Call me as soon as you get in!"

Her news is extraordinary. "I found my first cousin! His name is Jim Brown and he lives just ten miles from me. Can you believe it? He and his wife had us over for coffee and I stood outside their door just shaking before I rang the bell. You know what it's like. Jim has no idea what happened to my mother, she disappeared years ago, but I know you'll be excited by this. He has pages and pages on our family tree."

A family tree? *Our* family tree?

"He's documented our family back several generations. We even have a relative who died in the Civil War."

"Who? Where?"

She is excited, with so many thoughts overwhelming her that my normally detail-oriented birth mother cannot remember any details. "I should have written this all down. His name was... Edwin Brown. He died at... where was it? A place that begins with the letter 'A'."

I toss out the first name that leaps into my mind. "Antietam?"

"That's it! Antietam. Jim says he was a hero, that he died leading a charge or something. He was a captain in some kind of hat brigade."

"The Black Hats?"

"Yes!"

"Lenore," I take in a deep breath. "That's the Iron Brigade."

"You know about them?"

"I'll call you right back." I race upstairs to my office, pulling Catton's <u>Army of the Potomac</u> from a shelf and flip to the first page on Antietam. The battle took place on September 17, 1862 and the Iron Brigade was involved from the beginning. I scan the first paragraphs, grab two more books, and hurry toward the stairs to phone Lenore back when the antique photograph hanging in the hallway stops me in my tracks.

Tiff, wearing the uniform of a Union soldier, stares at me, sepia-toned, from the wall. A chill runs down my spine. When were we in Harper's Ferry? September 17th. How far is Harper's Ferry from Antietam? An inch on the map.

This photograph, the only one our son has ever asked for, was taken on the anniversary of Antietam, less than fifteen miles from the battlefield. I later learn that when Captain Edwin Arnold Brown died on September 17th, 1862, he had his pistol drawn and his sword held high - the exact two items Tiff had requested.

40

Edwin Arnold Brown gazes at me from a frame on my desk, his expression somber, as was the custom in 1861. Beside him in the photograph is a boy with neatly combed hair and an identical gaze, his five-year-old son Louie. Usually children stood stiffly for such portraits, but Louie makes a statement, leaning proudly into his Pa.

These are my ancestors.

The picture was taken before my third (great great great) grandfather joined the Union Army. Like many in the North, he felt it was his duty to honor the sacrifices made by his own great grandfathers in the Revolutionary War. I *know* he believed this because Lenore sends me Xeroxed copies of fifty-five letters Edwin wrote home to his wife during the War.

> *Dear Ruth,*
> *...know that I am trying to do what I can for the country of my birth, for the preservation of those rights and institutions established and made sacred by the sacrifice of our forefathers...*

In addition to Louie, there were two other children, a three-year-old son, Pier (Pie-Or), and little Hattie, not yet a year old. Edwin missed them terribly when he left Fond du Lac and joined the Sixth Wisconsin Volunteers. Almost every letter to Ruth ends, *"Kiss the babies for me."*

His best friend in the Union Army was Rufus Dawes. As fellow officers in the Sixth Wisconsin, the two developed a deep bond, and a handful of anecdotes, written down by Dawes and others from the regiment, document their friendship.

One anecdote tells of the time in the spring of 1862 when the Sixth Wisconsin marched into Virginia. Supplies were low and Edwin and Rufus hiked to the only house on the horizon to see if they could buy some food. Their knock on the door was answered by a pale woman with six small children. Rufus hinted they were starving and offered money for any scraps she might have, but the woman snapped that a Union general had exhausted her larder.

While Rufus spoke, Edwin gathered the woman's little children on his knees, telling them about his own children back home, and then he drew a bright medallion from his pocket inscribed, 'The War of 1861, Captain E.A. Brown, Sixth Wisconsin Volunteers' which he gave to the children as a gift. His gesture "melted the maternal heart" and the woman insisted they let her fix them some eggs.

After visiting that kitchen and holding those children, Edwin sank into a deep depression, evident in his subsequent letters home.

> *...Ruth, I have the blues severely... I have been living in the hope of a chance to visit but... I have no hope whatever in being able to get a furlough while the struggle lasts...*

In August of 1862, Dawes was on the battlefield to witness the day when Edwin and his company chased down a group of Confederate soldiers who were disguised as Union Calvary, "earning the first glory for the Sixth Wisconsin on the field." A week later, following the battle of Second Manassas, Edwin wrote his father that,

> *...We took prisoners who said... we drove the famous "Stonewall Brigade" off the field... this was the first time they ever turned their back to the foe. They asked if we were not Western troops, saying they knew we were not Yankees . . .*

Then, the Confederate Army invaded Maryland, hoping to force the Union into suing for peace. There would be no rest for the Sixth Wisconsin until the Rebels were forced back into Virginia. Edwin and Rufus and the rest of the Sixth marched toward Sharpsburg, a village bordering a creek named Antietam. He scribbled a note to Ruth, only the last page of which exists.

...the Rebels have earned their right to a separation by their ability + daring...Good bye and God's blessings be with you... Kiss the babies for me.

- Ed

This is his last known correspondence. Less than forty-eight hours later, on a Wednesday morning in the middle of September, during the bloodiest battle in American military history, my third great grandfather would die.

41

I have dreamed of knowing my ancestors. Now I immerse myself in the life and death of the first one I have a chance to really know. I search bookstores for everything I can find on the Iron Brigade and Antietam. With each book, I flip to the index first. If 'Brown, Capt. Edwin' is listed, I buy it.

Jon and the boys drive with me to Antietam National Battlefield on a gray November afternoon. Less than a mile from the park headquarters, the Miller farmhouse still stands. It was on this farm that a bullet ended Edwin's life, and if any terrain seems mournful, it is these barren fields.

On the night of September 16th, 1862, with their men sleeping in close columns, rifles ready at their sides, Edwin and Rufus and the other officers of the Sixth made coffee and softly sang songs. Was it Edwin who suggested they sing his favorite tune, "Benny Haven's Oh!"?

We bid a sad a-dieu,
our hearts with sorrow over-flow,
Our love's and rhymings had their source
at Benny Havens Oh!

What were Edwin's thoughts on that last night? I am certain as I stand on the ground where he died: he wanted to go home. I believe he sat beside the campfire thinking of his wife and children.

Was he prescient? Did he know what lay in store for him?

At dawn on September 17th, a heavy mist covered the ground as Union troops marched toward the cornfield in the distance. A hundred cannon thundered before them, limbs of trees, severed by shells, fell upon them, and smoke and shouts filled the air.

At Miller's farm, a fence blocked their advance, and Rufus ordered Edwin to take his company through a gate. Edwin, his sword raised, his pistol drawn, shouted the orders. "Company E, on the right by file into line!" Then Rufus saw him stuck down, shot through the mouth, and would later write, "his voice is silent forever."

That men can continue on after viewing such a sight (Edwin was, after all, Rufus's best friend) astounds me. A few days after the battle, Rufus would write his mother, "Captain Edwin A. Brown... my best friend in the regiment, was shot dead at Sharpsburg." But on the battlefield, after Edwin fell, Rufus and the rest of the Sixth Wisconsin continued on toward their horrible destiny in that cornfield, leaving their comrade behind.

> *Dear Son,*
> *...Our earnest prayer is that you have gone through the deadly contest safely... The excitement has been intense here since Thursday evening caused by the report that Lieut. Col. Bragg was killed on Wednesday...*
> *Your Affectionate Father, Isaac Brown*

Back in Fond du Lac, a cruel error played out. A telegram was sent to the Sixth Wisconsin Commander Edward Bragg's wife informing her that, "Your Husband was shot yesterday...will send him home by express." All Fond du Lac plunged into mourning for the loss of the regimental commander. But Edward Bragg was not dead.

Ruth was expressing her condolences at the Bragg home when a telegram arrived from Chicago, sent by the men who had gone to retrieve Bragg's casket. It stated simply: "The body is Capt. E. A. Brown instead of Bragg. Will be home tomorrow..." In this way, Ruth learned of her husband's death.

A large crowd met the train bearing Edwin's body at the Fond du Lac Depot and Ruth and the children led the cortege as it moved slowly to the tiny cemetery on her parents' farm. As the sun set, the casket was lowered into the ground. Edwin was finally 'home'.

Two decades later, at an Iron Brigade reunion, when Brigadier General John Gibbons called upon Edwin's old friends to sing "Benny Haven's", not one of them could do it. The last time they had sung that song together was the night before Edwin was killed, and they choked back tears, unable to utter a note. So Gibbons began the song alone, and one by one, Rufus and the other surviving members of the Sixth Wisconsin began to add their voices, their thoughts on Edwin, and the song reverberated through the building and echoed far out into the night.

Oh, Benny Havens, oh, Benny Havens, oh!
We'll sing our reminiscences of Benny Havens, oh!

Today, the only sound at Miller's Farm is the wind whistling across the empty fields. It is a god awful sound. Such a lonely place, this land. I came here to find Edwin Arnold Brown, to know him, but he is not here. He visited for a few hours, leaving his blood upon this ground, but he is gone. The only thing left of him on Earth were his children and a handful of his words in letters.

As I stand beside this empty farmhouse on Antietam Battlefield, I suddenly realize that I, too, play a part in the legacy of this man. He is my ancestor and I am his descendant, and like his son Louie in the photograph on my desk, I find myself leaning into Edwin, with pride.

42

Edwin's death made his wife, Ruth, old. Lenore's newfound cousin, Jim Brown, sends me a photograph of her, dressed in widow's black, her eyes empty, looking fifty, not twenty-five. In her own obituary many years later, she was quoted as telling friends that she never got over the shock of Edwin's death. "I was never my real self again."

She was the daughter of pioneers. Her parents, Edward and Harriet Pier, were Vermont farmers who emigrated West in search of better farm land, becoming the founding settlers of Fond du Lac, Wisconsin.

Oliver Pier	Elizabeth Webster	Eleazer Kendall	Sally
b. May 9, 1741	b. April 8, 1741	b. 1756 in Massachusetts	b. unknown
Fought in	Gr. granddaughter,	d. 1840 in Vermont	d. 1779
Revolutionary War	1st governor of Conn.		
d. 1805, VT	d. 1783 in Mass.		

Calvin Pier	Esther Evarts	Nathan Kendall	Betsy Stearns
b Feb. 22, 1780	b. April 18, 1784	b. 1779	b. April 12, 1785
d. 1856, Wis.	d. 1869, Fond du Lac	d. 1811	d. unknown

Edward Pier	Colwert Pier	Harriet Kendall	Fanna Kendall
b. 1807	b. 1810	b. 1810	b. unknown
m. Harriet Kendall	m. Fanny Kendall	Four children	died childless
d. 1877	d. 1856	d. 1864	d. 1837

Ruth Pier
b. 1837
m. Edwin Arnold Brown, 1851
Three children: Louie, Pier, Hattie
d. 1897

Ruth's father and uncle purchased a land claim at the south end of Lake Winnebago in 1836. The first winter at the cabin in the woods was brutal. A letter written by my great-great-great-great grandfather, Edward Pier, describes his mid-winter journey to bring supplies to the homestead from Green Bay.

... the snow was so strongly driven by the force of the wind, that I could only see a few feet... my horse dropped through the ice into the water... I put the lines around his neck and pulled him back on the ice, but it immediately broke, and when he went in again, he took me with him. I sprang on top of him... saw that he was gone, and I now started to find the only house in Fond du Lac County.

Of course, I was in great anxiety for fear I could not find it... My overcoat was frozen stiff, my boots filled with water... (reaching the cabin) was the only chance for my life.

The cattle had been out on the east side of the timber that day; and I will here say that I never was so glad in my life to see the tracks of a cow...

Edward followed the tracks straight to the cabin and survived to tell the tale. His wife, Harriet, made the journey down Lake Winnebago by longboat after the ice thawed that spring, carrying their youngest child, a four week old infant, in her arms.

Little House in the Big Woods was my favorite book when I learned to read. It tells the story of a small girl growing up in the Wisconsni wilderness. I checked it out of the Lafayette Library at least a half dozen times. I felt like it was my story.

The four-week-old infant Harriet Pier carried with her to the cabin in the woods, the first white baby in Wisconsin Territory, was Ruth, my great-great-great grandmother. She grew up in a little house in the big woods, listened to the wolves howl on long winter nights, tasted the sugar snow and breathed in the smell of hickory smoke curing bacon.

I feel I have known her all along.

43

On a large piece of paper, I make my long-sought-after family tree, carefully writing down each ancestor's name, date of birth, marriage and death, and anecdotes whenever possible.

Thomas Brown
b. Apr. 16, 1733 in Rhode Island.
d. March 11, 1814, New Berlin, New York.
Revolutionary War Soldier. Answered the alarm, April 19, 1775.

Armed with information from Jim Brown, I can list thirteen generations of ancestors on my family tree, all the way back to John Browne, a shipbuilder who came to Massachusetts in 1632. An Assistant of Plymouth Colony's Court, he helped found the Massachusetts towns of Taunton and Rehoboth and Swansea. I find several books on him at the library, and the more I read, the more I realize: I already *know* him.

In my office, I pull a mauve-covered book from a shelf. I was assigned this book of essays on colonial history two decades ago while a student at Cal Berkeley. Only one chapter is highlighted: an essay about Plymouth Colony written by John Demos of Yale.

> *...apprentices (were often)...young boys and girls, 'bound out' for a specific term of years...a virtual deed of adoption... Samuel Eddy arranged apprenticeships for three of his sons, at ages six, seven, and nine. Two of them went to the same man, Mr. John Browne of Rehoboth...*

I remember this article. It intrigued me because it spoke about the first adoptions in America. Yet, as I read it now, there is another reason for me to be intrigued: Mr. John Browne of Rehoboth is my tenth great grandfather.

I not only know John Browne, I know his son James. In college, I wrote a paper about James, whose life was spared by the Indian chief, King Philip.

James had been sent by the governors of Massachusetts and Rhode Island as an emissary to King Philip in the hopes of avoiding bloodshed. The warriors of King Philip's tribe wanted to kill him, but Philip's late father, Wannamasoit, had charged him to show kindness to John Browne and his heirs, and so the warrior chief spared James Browne's life.

John and James Browne are not important figures in American history, yet I was drawn to their stories. In discovering my connection to them, I wonder: are we somehow unwittingly attracted to our ancestors when they cross our paths?

Cousin Jim has provided me with a history of the Browne men, but little about the women they married. Who were they? At the American Antiquarian Society, a library of American history in Massachusetts, I seek whatever information I can find about them.

James Browne married Lydia Howland. I stare at the symbol beside her name in a book. (⚓.) I know what this symbol means. Lydia Howland was a Mayflower descendant.

I am a Mayflower descendant.

Lydia's father, John Howland, was twenty-eight years old when he sailed to America aboard the Mayflower in 1620. During the voyage, passengers weren't allowed up on deck. When a storm hit, conditions in the hold grew wretched, and John Howland snuck topside for some fresh air. A wave hit the ship and washed him overboard. Adrift in the frigid Atlantic waters, Howland managed to grab hold of a halyard trailing from the ship. Hanging on as the rope lost slack, he was dragged several fathoms under water until sailors on board used a boat hook to fish him out of the sea.

Governor Bradford later wrote, "He was sundry sick for many days." But John Howland survived, which is a good thing, because he hadn't fathered any children yet, so I wouldn't be here, and neither would Franklin Roosevelt or Winston Churchill or Humphrey Bogart who are also descendants of John Howland and his future wife, fellow Mayflower passenger, Elizabeth Tilley.

I drive toward Plymouth on Highway 44, a route that John Browne himself mapped out three and a half centuries ago. I try to imagine him on horseback, making his way through these woods, across these fields, on his way to Plymouth Court. A mailman zooms past me, the lights atop his metallic blue sports car flashing, breaking my reverie.

The streets of Plymouth are clogged with tourists. I follow the crowd past the replica of the Mayflower to Plymouth Rock. John Howland's boot prints were washed away centuries ago, and his body has long since turned to dust. But he was here.

Three miles south is Plimoth Plantation, a recreation of the original Pilgrim settlement with actors dressed in costumes of the day. There is only one person I am here to see and she is walking toward me, alone on the path leading to a small house with a thatched roof. "Excuse me," I say. "Are you Elizabeth Howland?"

"Aye missus, that's me." I strike up a conversation with the young actress portraying my tenth great grandmother. We talk of her voyage to America aboard the Mayflower when she was fourteen, of her parents who died that first spring in America, of her husband and young children. I feel a blurring of time and reality, as if I am actually hearing Elizabeth's own words. The young actress portraying her speaks with such an ease and sincerity that I feel I have entered my ancestor's life for a moment, and it is a good life.

Elizabeth is one of my foremothers, as is Margaret Denison, who is listed on Jim Brown's family tree as my eighth great grandmother. All I know about Margaret is that she married James Browne in 1678, but her last name is familiar. In college, I wrote an essay about a man named George Denison who captured Canonchet, chief of the Narragansett tribe, during King Philip's War. I wonder if Margaret is related to him. On the very first page of a book on the Denisons at the A.A.S. Library, I learn that Margaret was, in fact, George Denison's daughter. When I wrote about the capture of Canonchet twenty years ago, I was writing about my own ninth great grandfather.

The book also says that the family homestead still stands on the site in Connecticut where George and his wife Ann settled in 1652. I decide to see it on my way home from Plymouth. The wood-shingled house, sturdy and inviting, is a touchstone for all Denisons. I walk inside, underneath the sign that says, "Welcome."

A distant cousin leads me on a tour, ending in a small cottage which houses a gift shop. There, I discover the <u>Denison Genealogy</u>, and browse its contents. I'm surprised to read that two children, given up by Denisons for adoption, are listed as family because, of course, they *are* Denison descendants. Oddly, it is only when I read these entries that I realize my name and Lenore's would be included in this tome. It is a nice feeling.

On my way out of town, I stop to see the Denison Memorial at Elm Grove Cemetery. George is buried in Hartford where he died, but Ann's remains were moved to this site by descendants who erected a monument to the family. Her gravestone stands, tilted and sinking in the earth, beside the obelisk which reads:

George Denison. Founder of the Denison family.
Died October 23, 1694, aged 74.
This stone is erected by his descendants in 1856.
Ann B. His wife died September 16, 1712 age 97.

I am surprised at how this monument affects me. It makes me angry. *Ann* was a first settler and founder, too. They unearthed her bones to move them to this spot, yet she's barely acknowledged for her contribution. This pioneer woman bore seven children in an untamed land without support of family, neighbors, or midwives. "I know what you did," I say to the sinking gravestone. "I am alive because of you."

The Howlands. The Tilleys. The Brownes. The Denisons. Like a kid collecting baseball cards, I become obsessed with collecting my 'nth' great grandparents. I spend hours at the kitchen table making family trees of my newfound ancestors. When my friend Barb calls, I tell her about my wonderful foremothers. I tell her about Elizabeth Tilley Howland and the Mayflower.

Barb stops me. "I'm a Howland descendant, too."

I'm certain she's mistaken. Descending from a Mayflower passenger is something unusual, right? Only twenty-six passengers left descendants. But Barb sends me Xeroxed pages from a book that proves she is a Howland descendant, just like me.

Then I talk to Kathy, my roommate from before I married Jon, and she says, "I'm a Howland, too." So is a man I meet at a luncheon in Maryland. A woman I talk to at a funeral in California. A doctor I meet while giving a speech in New England. Everyone seems to be related to this one couple. Maybe I'm not so special after all. Kathy puts it all in perspective for me.

"If you're related to Howland," I tell her, "that means you're related to FDR and Churchill and a bunch of other famous people."

"That's interesting," says Kathy. "But I'm more excited to find out I'm related to you."

I walk around smiling for an entire week.

I share what I learn about the Pilgrims with Jim Brown. We owe him so much, and now I feel I can give him something back. I call to tell him about Elizabeth Howland and James Browne and the Massachusetts mailman in the metallic blue sports car.

Lenore calls me a week later. "Jean. I have some awful news. Jim Brown just died."

I catch my breath. Impossible.

"He got sick, a rare virus. It was very sudden."

I can't believe it. I just sent him pages about the Howlands. He sent me a card and signed it, "Your cousin, Jim." How can he be gone?

We have known him less than two months, but this long-lost cousin gave us one of the greatest gifts of our lives. He gave us our family tree. I hold on tightly to the torch he passed. He was a griot, like me, and I will continue the search he began for our ancestors. It is the only way I can ever thank him.

44

Jon takes a new job in Washington, D.C., and we have lived in our brand new home in Maryland for only three weeks when he has to go out of town on business in early December. The night he's due to return, I put the boys to bed, pull out bags of Christmas presents to wrap, and head to the garage for the box of wrapping paper. The moment the garage door closes behind me, I know I've made a mistake. The door is locked.

I chuckle. Even though I'm barefoot, wearing only black stretch pants and a long-sleeve t-shirt with the temperature hovering around freezing, I'm not concerned. Why worry? The kids are right upstairs. Who needs a key?

I ring the doorbell once and wait a moment to hear them stir. Nothing. I ring it again and put my ear to the door to listen for their little footsteps bounding down the stairs. Nothing. I ring the bell again and again, then try the knocker.

The only other occupied house on the street is dark, the new owners out of town. We have no other neighbors on our cul-de-sac, only raw foundations and framed walls, and I know no one in the bordering neighborhood. As I ring our doorbell a hundred times, I'm no longer chuckling.

I take a ladder from the garage and lean it against the side of the house below the boys' bedrooms. A certified acrophobic, I creep up the rungs, covering the bold yellow DO NOT SIT OR STAND HERE warning on the top step with my bare feet and, on tiptoe, rap on the window. I can see Tiff and Jonathon sleeping just five feet away. They don't stir. I get a screwdriver from the garage and use its hard plastic handle on the window pane. "Tap, tap, tap!" Nothing. Next, I try Tiff's baseball bat. "Wham! Wham! Wham!" I balance on the top step, pounding on the windows which don't break or even crack. Amazing. And equally amazing, neither Jonathon nor Tiff budge.

By now, I have been outside for forty-five minutes. Jon's due home at eleven, an hour away. I need to get warm. Rummaging through boxes in the garage, I find a Santa Claus hat for my head, a pair of cross country ski boots for my sockless feet, and an old blanket we use when we're raking the yard which I wrap around me, its dead leaves scratching the back of my neck. I am not very happy.

I ring the doorbell a thousand times. I throw rocks at the window. I shout my sons' names. They do not hear me.

An hour creeps by and there is no sign of Jon. I look longingly at the dark-windowed houses just past the end of our court. If I knew any of the people living in them, they might invite me in and give me some hot chocolate and socks. But I know no one and cannot imagine walking up to one of those houses and ringing the doorbell in my Santa hat and ski boots and leafy blanket.

The temperature drops lower and lower. I wonder if I will die before Jon gets home. Midnight passes, and still he doesn't arrive. What if his flight was canceled? The boys will come downstairs in the morning and find me frozen on the front stoop like a decorative doorstop.

At one thirty, Jon pulls in the driveway and flips on his high beams. A strange person wearing a Santa Claus hat is sitting on his front porch. "Merry Christmas," I growl as he comes up the walkway. He does not look at me in awe after I tell him the story. He looks at the windows in awe. "These triple panes are amazing."

I take a bath and as the hot water spills over my tingling toes, I think about John and Elizabeth Howland. I bet the Pilgrims knew all of their neighbors. I bet they never sat outside without socks on during the week after Thanksgiving.

"Looks like snow," Jon says in January, peering out the window up at the sky. A blizzard descends upon us, two monster storms, one right after the other. Washington, D.C. does not have the equipment to deal with four foot drifts and the streets remain filled with snow for days, impassable. Trucks cannot reach the grocery store, but a skeleton crew keeps it open, and Jon shoulders a backpack and treks off to get supplies. There are no perishable goods, no fresh fruits or vegetables, no meat, no milk. He brings home pretzels and wine and Cheerios and powdered milk and we have a feast.

We strap on cross-country skis and traverse our neighborhood. People wave at us from their windows and come out of their houses. "Hello," they say, introducing themselves. "Do you need anything?"

"No," we smile. "But thank you for asking."

We are snowbound for eight days. There is no school, no life outside this community where people walk from door to door, checking on each other. This is what it was like for the Pilgrims, I think. I like it.

Then, like magic, the sun comes out and the land heats up and the snow disappears overnight. Jonathon asks, "When the snow melts, where does all the white go?"

It is a good question. We take him to Great Falls on the Potomac River and show him that the white snow becomes white water. The waves on the river are immense, rushing by us with tremendous force. Thousands of people come to witness the raw power of the water, and later, thousands will volunteer to help clean up the wreckage left by the flood, shoveling mud and rebuilding the canal trails.

As the waters recede, everything returns to normal in our neighborhood. We no longer walk up to each other's doors and ask if anyone needs help. We stay within the walls of our own homes. But I now know: all I have to do is knock.

45

"Gees, could you go a little slower?" I say to the lumbering old truck several cars in front of us, creeping up the gentle grade.

"Maybe it's too old to go any faster." Tiff is ten, and far too mature sometimes for my liking.

Mile after mile the truck plods on and behind us on the two lane highway in upstate New York, a long line of frustrated drivers begins to form. I look at my watch and shake my head. There are gravestones I had planned to locate before sunset, places I need to be.

At a stoplight where the highway bisects another, I slide along the shoulder past the cars in front of me, pull even with the offending truck at the head of the line, my intention to turn right, pull into the gas station kitty corner to us, and zip up the hill ahead of the truck.

The light is still red as I turn. I never look left, my vision obscured by the old truck, so I do not see the big rig barreling into the intersection at sixty miles an hour. I do not see the truck until it is an inch from my door, parallel with my car. The driver does not honk for he has no time to honk, only a fraction of a second to respond, pulling into the empty opposing lane.

Whoosh! The cushion of air between our two vehicles pushes my little rental car right off the road. I hit the brakes, kicking up gravel, throwing my arm instinctively across Tiff. "It's okay, Mom," he says as I start to cry.

No, it's not okay. I have been distracted by ancestors long buried, and have come within an inch of planting us both into the ground.

It is strange obsession, this hunting for graves. We have been in New Berlin, New York, the village where Edwin Arnold Brown was born in 1832. Tiff, my reluctant companion on this journey, does not share my enthusiasm for visiting the land of our ancestors and discovering their final resting places. He yawns while I speak with the New Berlin town clerk.

"I wasn't able to find a stone for Lydia Arnold Brown," she says.

"But see these obituaries." I hold out two newspaper articles about Lydia's death. "Both list her as being buried at Main Street Cemetery."

The woman shakes her head as she glances at the obits. "I walked the entire cemetery last week and couldn't find her."

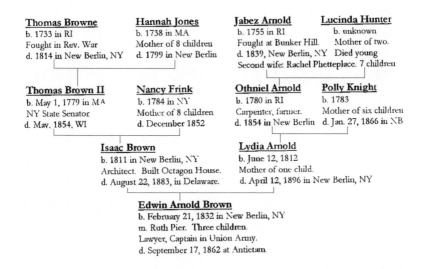

Thomas Browne
b. 1733 in RI
Fought in Rev. War
d. 1814 in New Berlin, NY

Hannah Jones
b. 1738 in MA
Mother of 8 children
d. 1799 in New Berlin

Jabez Arnold
b. 1755 in RI
Fought at Bunker Hill.
d. 1839, New Berlin, NY

Lucinda Hunter
b. unknown
Mother of two.
Died young
Second wife: Rachel Phetteplace. 7 children

Thomas Brown II
b. May 1, 1779 in MA
NY State Senator
d. May. 1854, WI

Nancy Frink
b. 1784 in NY
Mother of 8 children
d. December 1852

Othniel Arnold
b. 1780 in RI
Carpenter, farmer.
d. 1854 in New Berlin

Polly Knight
b. 1783
Mother of six children
d. Jan. 27, 1866 in NB

Isaac Brown
b. 1811 in New Berlin, NY
Architect. Built Octagon House.
d. August 22, 1883, in Delaware.

Lydia Arnold
b. June 12, 1812
Mother of one child.
d. April 12, 1896 in New Berlin, NY

Edwin Arnold Brown
b. February 21, 1832 in New Berlin, NY
m. Ruth Pier. Three children.
Lawyer, Captain in Union Army.
d. September 17, 1862 at Antietam.

Edwin Arnold Brown's mother, Lydia, died on my birthday a hundred years ago. I found his father's grave in Delaware and used a stiff hairbrush to scrape away the years of grit and decay in order to decipher the words.

Isaac Brown, 1811-1883
Sleep thou and the dawn shall find thee,
On that bright beloved shore.

Now I walk the rows of a cemetery in New Berlin, hoping to find Edwin's mother, Lydia, while Tiff remains in the car, reading a book. When I race over to tell him I have found Jabez Arnold, he is not interested in seeing his seventh great grandfather's stone, even after I remind him of the story.

Jabez, Lydia's grandfather, fought at Bunker Hill, the first major battle of the Revolutionary War. Before the battle, his brother Othniel had a premonition he would be killed and, worried about his fiancee, Rachel, had begged Jabez, "If I am killed, will you promise to marry Rachel?"

"Nothing's going to happen to you," Jabez had said.

"I want to know Rachel will be taken care of." Othniel persisted until his brother agreed. When the third wave of Redcoats cleared the breech works, Othniel was struck by a British bullet, and after the war, Jabez kept his word: he married Rachel Phetteplace.

Edwin lived in New Berlin as a small boy, and as I stand beside Jabez's grave, I imagine Edwin listening to his great grandfather tell stories about Bunker Hill. I remember his letter home to Ruth, explaining why he was leaving her and the children to go off to war: *Know that I am trying to do what I can... (to preserve) those rights and institutions established and made sacred by the sacrifice of our forefathers....*

I find other members of the Arnold family, but I cannot find a stone for Lydia anywhere. Where is she? My eyes drift to a place near Jabez's grave, to a tangled vine, a mound of dirt and I see a stone, broken in two, embedded in the ground, with it's blank sides facing out. My fingers dig into the earth, until I loosen a piece and pull it out. I wipe away soil and read:

YDIA ARNOL

It is her! I have found Edwin's mother, my fourth great grandmother. The second piece is heavier, deeper. I bend my knees and lift, and there is the rest.

L   D

Wife of Isaac Brown
Died April 12, 1896
Aged 84 Years

I clean the two pieces as best I can and lay them together, like a broken love charm, now whole, for the world to see. When I show Tiff the rescued stone, he stands quietly for a few moments, trying to mollify me, to be respectful, but he does not understand this pursuit. He does not want to find a gravestone. He wants to find a Burger King.

Early the next morning, we drive to the farm that belonged to Edwin's paternal grandparents, Thomas and Hannah Brown. A letter I found at the Norwich Library tells me vaguely where they are buried. "Walk across the cow pasture off Great Brook Road, over the fence, across the brook, up the hill, to the clump of trees surrounded by the stone wall."

"More gravestones?" Tiff asks, rolling his eyes. He pulls out his book. "I'm going to stay here and read, okay?"

"Okay," I say. "Honk the horn if you need me."

It is foggy and damp as I set off across the dew-laced cow pasture in my khaki shorts and Joan and David leather oxfords. Big mistake. The shoes are instantly soaked and caked with mud.

I can barely see, the fog is so thick. I squish back and forth across the pasture, trying to find a way through the fence. Finally, I see the break in the wire, the brook, and the old trail worn on the other side.

I cross the stream and walk up the gentle hill, straining to find the landmarks that were mentioned in the letter. There are some trees to my left, but no stone wall. I keep going all the way to the top of the long hill. Nothing. My son is a mile away, back on the farm road, reading in our rental car. How long have I been out here? An hour?

In defeat, I head back down the old path, my Joan and David's squishing loudly. The morning sun begins to burn away the mist and suddenly the land comes into focus. I pause at the clump of trees I passed on my way up the hill, trying to see through the fortress of thistles and brambles, and literally stumble across a stone wall obscured by the undergrowth. This is it!

Why did I wear shorts? My legs are scratched and bloodied by thorns as I push my way toward the center of the thicket where the vines thin slightly, and I can see gravestones, reddish and tall, guarded by some sinister looking bushes.

Hannah died here in 1799, Thomas in 1814. I rest against their stones, catching my breath. I am a griot. I know their history. Thomas was a sergeant in the Revolutionary War. Hannah gave birth to five sons and five daughters. I place my hand where their own children did, upon these stones, the writing now almost illegible. Traces of my ancestors are being washed away by the rain. I have found them just in time.

I jerk my head at the sound of a car horn. Tiff! I race back through the stickers, down the ancient trail, splashing across the brook, over the barbed wire fence, and through the field. "You okay?" I huff when I open the car door.

"Can we look for a Burger King now?"

An hour later, my mind on ancestors, I pull out into the intersection of two highways and almost collide with a truck.

My favorite book when I was learning to read was Laura Ingalls Wilder's Little House In The Big Woods. I read it so many times I can remember, verbatim, certain sections. At the very end of the book, as Laura watched her parents in the firelight, her father playing his fiddle, her mother knitting, she thought to herself, "*This is now.*" And she was glad that the house and the music and her parents were 'now'. "*They could not be forgotten, she thought, because now is now. It can never be a long time ago.*"

I look at my son beside me in the car and pull him into my arms, not because he needs a hug, but because I do. I almost forgot. This is now. It is more important than anything written on a stone.

46

Lenore's birth father is dead.

She finds his name listed in the Social Security Death Index at the Mormon Library in Minneapolis. He died in 1973, over twenty-five years ago. "Here's this person I don't even know, but I feel sick to learn he's gone." Her voice cracks. "My father is dead."

Knowing the date and location of his death, I locate his grave and, at Lenore's urging, on a trip to California I drive to the cemetery. It seems unfair that I am visiting him first. This is Lenore's father, not mine, but she tells me, "Go, find him." So I do.

Georg, my grandfather, is buried on a gentle slope with mountains in the distance, his inscription:

Beloved son and father.
Always in our smiles and hearts.

"He was loved," I tell Lenore.

All along, I knew the search would end this way. Georg would have been in his eighties now, so the odds of finding either he or Mary alive have been against us all along. But Lenore calls a week later. "She's not dead!"

"Who?"

"My mother! I went back to the Mormon Library and typed Mary Frances Brown into the Social Security Death Index. I was so afraid I would find out she was dead, too, but she wasn't listed."

I don't point out to Lenore that Mary might have been listed by a married name in the SSI index. I don't tell her I think she's never going to find her mother.

"She's out there, Jean," Lenore says, adamant. "I'm never giving up."

Months later, she manages to locate Mary's nephew, Glenn, but even he has no idea what happened to his Aunt Mary. "She married someone with an unusual last name back in the fifties," he says. "It sounded like McCloskey, but that's not it."

"You don't remember?"

"The last time I saw her was in 1962 at my mother's funeral."

"Do you have any pictures of her?"

"No." There is a pause. "But I can tell you a little bit about her. My aunt was an Army nurse who served overseas in World War Two. She had three children, a girl and two boys."

Lenore has a sister and two brothers.

We look up every derivation of the name McCloskey we can think of. McCloskie. McCoskie. MacCasey. McClossen. We call people throughout the United States whose names are even remotely similar. "Hi. We are looking for a Mary Frances Brown who was a nurse in WWII."

I put Lenore in touch with the author of <u>How to Find Anyone Who Is or Has Been in the Military</u>, and he is able to retrieve Mary's service record, but nothing more. He suggests that Lenore contact Social Security directly. I fear all she will find is another dead end, another blank record. But I am wrong.

I know even before Lenore says the words that something wonderful has happened. Her voice is beaming. "I found her, Jean! I found her! My mother is collecting Social Security benefits. They can't give me her address, but my mother is alive!" It sinks in. My birth mother's birth mother is alive. Lenore's mother is alive. My grandmother is alive!

Her name is Mary Brown *Miklosey*, a spelling I never thought to try. Social Security will not give Lenore her address, but they will forward one letter written by a child to a parent.

"You must be very careful what you write," I caution Lenore. "We know nothing about her. We don't know if anyone in her family knows about you."

Lenore spends days crafting the letter, reading me draft upon draft until she is done.

Dear Mother,

It's been a long, long time since we've seen each other. In fact, it was in Portland, Oregon. Remember? I have eight grown children and fourteen grandchildren. Please know that I don't want anything from you outside of hearing from you... I hope you are well, and that life has been good for you.

With love, Lenore

A friend of mine, who has facilitated thousands of reunions, cautions us there's only a ten percent chance that Mary will respond. "I don't mean to be discouraging," she says, "but it's been my experience that people in their eighties and nineties frequently feel, 'I've kept this secret this long, I'll just see you in heaven'."

I worry about Lenore. What will it do to her if she's rejected? A week passes, then another. We talk every day, reassuring each other that sending this letter to an eighty-year-old stranger was the right thing to do. "Even if you never hear from her," I say, "let's hope your letter gave her some peace."

"You know, that's what I'm feeling," says Lenore. "At peace. I know my mother has read my words."

My birth mother is sixty-one years old, but in many ways, she has just been reborn.

47

"Jean." I do not recognize the voice on the phone. It is Lenore and she is sobbing. I fear the worst. Something has happened to someone in the family. It is the dead of winter, mid-February, and the roads in Minnesota are icy. Several moments pass before Lenore is able to say, "I got a letter." Her voice is shaking. "I went down to the mailbox and there it was. I couldn't believe it."

"You mean... from Mary?"

"Yes. I got a letter from my mother. You have a grandmother, Jean."

I am flooded with feelings. Reunions no longer make me numb. They make me feel like I've received an electric shock. Zing! Every limb tingles. "Oh my god! What does she say?"

"I don't know. I'm too afraid to open the envelope."

I laugh, now, wishing I could be beside my birth mother to give her a hug. "Well, I suppose you don't ever have to open it. You could just frame the envelope. But then, you'll never know what she has to say."

I feel Lenore smile a thousand miles away. She takes a deep breath. "I'm so afraid. What if I've upset her? What if she doesn't want anything to do with me?"

"It'll be okay."

"What if she rejects me?"

"Then you've got me."

There is silence for a long time. Then Lenore says, "We're going to do this together." I hear her carefully tearing the envelope open. My birth mother is about to read the first words she has ever heard from her mother. "Are you there Jean?"

"I'm here as long as you need me."

"Okay." She clears her throat. "This is what she says."

The old woman opens the mailbox and retrieves a pile of mail. She is eighty-years-old, but her step is light as she returns to the house. She walked ten thousand miles between her seventieth birthday and her eightieth, and she has been trying to decide what to do for an encore.

She places the pile of mail on the dining room table and leafs through it. Most of it is for her son and his family, but there is a letter for her from Social Security, a thick envelope. She decides it must have something to do with her benefits, but inside is a second envelope, the address on it handwritten. "To: Mary Frances Brown, c/o Social Security." She does not recognize the handwriting. Why on earth would Social Security be sending her a letter from someone else? She hesitates for a moment, then tears open the flap.

The letter inside is typed.

"Dear Mother, It's been a long, long time since we've seen each other."

Dear Mother? For a moment, she is confused. Then she realizes: this is her daughter. She rereads the line.

"It's been a long, long time since we've seen each other. In fact, it was in Portland, Oregon. Remember?"

Oh yes, she remembers. For sixty years, she has pushed thoughts of that baby away. She is not someone who dwells on the past, but she has not forgotten. She feels sudden anxiety, fear. After all these years, she has been found out. What will her other children say? What will they do? Yet, she also feels pure joy to learn that her first child is still alive.

She retreats with the letter into her room and locks the door. Only then does she let the tears fall. They do not cease for a long time.

sunlight

My Family Tree

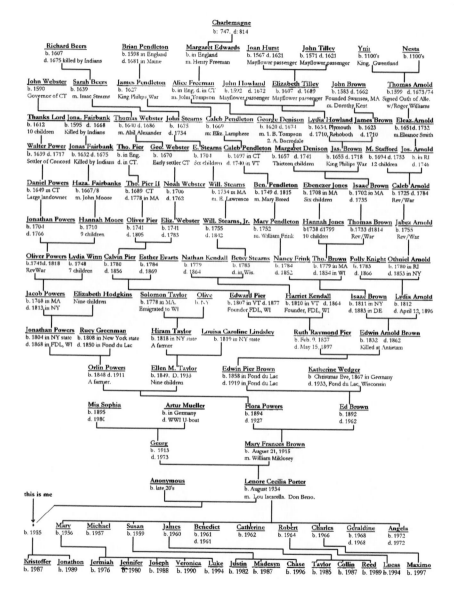

Charlemagne
b: 747. d: 814

Richard Beers b.1607 d. 1675 killed by Indians

Brian Pendleton b. 1598 in England d. 1681 in Maine

Margaret Edwards b. in England m. Henry Freeman

Joan Hurst b. 1567 d. 1621 Mayflower passenger

John Tilley b. 1571 d. 1621 Mayflower passenger

Ynir b. 1100's King. Gwendland

Nesta b. 1100's

John Webster b. 1590 Governor of CT

Sarah Beers b. 1639 m. Isaac Stearns

James Pendleton b. 1627 King Philips War

Alice Freeman b. in Eng. d. in CT m. John Tompson

John Howland b. 1592 d. 1672 Mayflower passenger

Elizabeth Tilley b. 1607 d. 1689 Mayflower passenger

John Brown b. 1583 d. 1662 Founded Swansea, MA m. Dorothy Kent

Thomas Arnold b.1599 d. 1673/74 Signed Oath of Alle. w/Roger Williams

Thanks Lord b. 1612 10 children

Jona. Fairbank b. 1595 d. 1668 Killed by Indians

Thomas Webster b. 1640 d. 1686 m. Abil Alexander

John Stearns b. 1675 d. 1734

Caleb Pendleton b. 1669

George Denison b. 1620 d. 1674 m: Eliz. Lamphere m. 1. B. Tompson 2. A. Borrodale

Lydia Howland b. 1634. Plymouth d. 1710, Rehoboth

James Brown b. 1623 d. 1710

Eleaz. Arnold b. 1651 d.1732 m.Eleanor Smith

Walter Power b. 1639 d. 1717 Settler of Concord

Jonas Fairbank b. 1632 d. 1675 Killed by Indians

Tho. Pier b. in Eng. d. in CT.

Geo. Webster b. 1670 Early settler CT

E. Stearns b. 1704 Six children

Caleb Pendleton b. 1697 in CT d. 1740 in VT

Margaret Denison b. 1657 d. 1741 Thirteen children

Jas. Brown b. 1655 d. 1718 King Philips War

M. Stafford b. 1694 d. 1753 12 children

Jos. Arnold b. in RI d. 1746

Daniel Powers b. 1649 in CT Large landowner

Haza. Fairbanks b. 1667/8 m. John Moore

Tho. Pier II b. 1689 CT d. 1778 in MA

Noah Webster b. 1706 d. 1762

Will. Stearns b. 1734 in MA m. E. Lawrence

Ben. Pendleton b. 1708 in MA Six children

Ebenezer Jones b. 1708 in MA

Isaac Brown b. 1702 in MA d. 1735

Caleb Arnold b. 1725 d. 1784 Rev/War

Jonathan Powers b. 1704 d. 1766

Hannah Moore b. 1710 9 children

Oliver Pier b. 1741 d. 1805

Eliz. Webster b. 1741 d. 1783

Will. Stearns, Jr. b. 1755 d. 1842

Mary Pendleton b. 1752 m. William Frink

Hannah Jones b1738 d1799

Thomas Brown b.1733 d.1814 Rev/War

Jabez Arnold b. 1755 Rev/War

Oliver Powers b.1741 d. 1818 Rev War

Lydia Winn b. 1748 7 children

Calvin Pier b. 1780 d. 1856

Esther Evarts b. 1784 d. 1869

Nathan Kendall b. 1779 d. 1864

Betsy Stearns b. 1785 d. in Wis.

Nancy Frink b. 1784 d. 1852

Tho. Brown b. 1779 in MA d. 1854 in WI

Polly Knight b. 1783 d. 1866

Othniel Arnold b. 1780 in RI d. 1853 in NY

Jacob Powers b. 1768 in MA d. 1813 in NY

Elizabeth Hodgkins Nine children

Solomon Taylor b. 1778 in MA. Emigrated to WI

Olive b. NY

Edward Pier b. 1807 in VT d. 1877 Founder FDL, WI

Harriet Kendall b. 1810 in VT d. 1864 Founder, FDL, WI

Isaac Brown b. 1811 in NY d. 1883 in DE

Lydia Arnold b. 1812 d. April 13, 1896

Jonathan Powers b. 1804 in NY state d. 1868 in FDL, WI

Rucy Greenman b. 1808 in New York state d. 1850 in Fond du Lac

Hiram Taylor b. 1818 in NY state A farmer

Louisa Caroline Lindsley b. 1819 in NY state

Ruth Raymond Pier b. Feb. 9, 1837 d. May 15, 1897

Edwin Arnold Brown b. 1832 d. 1862 Killed at Antietam

Orlin Powers b. 1848 d. 1911 A farmer.

Ellen M. Taylor b. 1849. D. 1933 Nine children

Edwin Pier Brown b. 1858 in Fond du Lac d. 1919 in Fond du Lac

Katherine Wedger b Christmas Eve, 1867 in Germany d. 1933, Fond du Lac, Wisconsin

Mia Sophia b. 1895 d. 1980

Artur Mueller b. in Germany d. WWI U-boat

Flora Powers b. 1894 d. 1927

Ed Brown b. 1892 d. 1962

Georg b. 1913 d. 1973

Mary Frances Brown b. August 21, 1915 m. William Miklosey

Anonymous b. late 20's

Lenore Cecilia Porter b. August 1934 m. Lou Iacarella. Don Beno.

this is me

b. 1955

Mary b. 1956

Michael b. 1957

Susan b. 1959

James b. 1960

Benedict b. 1961 d. 1961

Catherine b. 1962

Robert b. 1964

Charles b. 1966

Geraldine b. 1968 d. 1968

Angela b. 1972 d. 1972

Kristoffer b. 1987

Jonathon b. 1989

Jermiah b. 1976

Jennifer b. 1980

Joseph b. 1988

Veronica b. 1990

Luke b. 1994

Justin b. 1982

Madesyn b. 1987

Chase b. 1996

Taylor b. 1985

Collin b. 1987

Reed b. 1989

Lucas b.1994

Maximo b. 1997

48

Dear Lenore:

I am sorry for the delay in writing you but I had to come to terms with a part of my life that is in the distant past... Not answering immediately does not mean that I have no desire to communicate with you and thereby deny your existence. Never that!

I was encouraged to present you for adoption for I had no way to care for you... the only thing I could do was pray you would be safe. No one else in my family knows what happened to me over 60 years ago. I have been a widow for 25 years... I would ask you - please don't telephone this house at the present time. I will welcome correspondence...

With love that has never been expressed, I am,

Your mother

As Lenore reads her mother's letter to me over the phone, a remarkable thing happens: her voice changes. Lenore has always been tentative, even timid, when she speaks. Now, I hear strength for the first time, as if, in an instant, a wound of six decades is repaired.

Immediately, Lenore writes back.

What joy your letter gave me! I truly understand what a shock it was to receive my letter... After I heard from my own birth daughter, it sent me into a kind of time warp. It's hard to relive the past sometimes. Please know that I care how you are...

Dear Lenore:

I lit a candle for us this morning at Mass - one of those big ones that will last for a few days... Pray for me that I will have the courage to inform my children that the lost has been found...

Dear Mary,

Here we are - reaching across the expanse of years. The letter I received
from you yesterday made my heart sing!

Lenore and Mary meet through written words, and Mary begins to know me, her oldest grandchild, the same way when Lenore sends her a copy of Birthright. My grandmother, whom I have never known, reads my book about reunions while she is experiencing her own. Did I write it for her?

Lenore is ecstatic, yet also afraid. "I feel terrified that I'll never get to meet her or even talk to her on the phone."

Mary's hesitancy about Lenore phoning is due to the fact that she lives with her son, and he does not know about his long lost sister. But Mary takes a brave step: she tells him. This takes courage. She is eighty years old and risks the most important relationships in her life to acknowledge Lenore. Her fears of incurring disapproval evaporate when her son asks, "Are you happy?"

"Oh yes! I can't begin to describe it."

"Then, that's all that matters."

The very next day, Mary calls her daughter for the first time. "Lenore? It's your mother calling."

"Her voice is beautiful," Lenore tells me. "I am just so happy."

So is Mary.

My dear Lenore - (After we spoke) my mood immediately soared on high
as though I could easily "trip the light fantastic" as a very old saying
goes... Sometimes, especially when I have retired to my room in the
evening, I just sit quietly and reflect on the events of the past weeks and
how they have changed my life. For the better, I assure you!

Lenore tells me, "It's your turn. Write her."

I have held back, knowing from experience that the two of them need time to get to know each other without the distraction of the rest of us. "Don't you think it's too soon?"

"No. Write her."

> *Dear Mary,*
> *I have not had a grandmother since I was very young... I would*
> *love to know you, to hear your story. I would like to just hear*
> *your voice...*

I am doing dishes when the phone rings. "Jean? It's your grandmother." She sounds like she's fifty, not eighty. "Grandma?"

"Yes. That sounds so nice."

"Grandma." I could say it a thousand times and never get tired of it. After her call, I write her a ten page letter detailing our family history. My grandmother knows little about her ancestors, and is excited to learn more.

> *My dear Jean, Many thanks! It's great to have such helpful, loving and*
> *capable descendants!*
>
> > *Love you!*   *Grandmom*

Two months have passed when Mary calls Lenore to say, "It's time." She is ready to meet her daughter, face-to-face. They choose neutral territory, a hotel in Chicago where Lenore and Don will be attending a convention.

"What if she doesn't like me?" Lenore says before leaving for the airport.

"Just get on that plane," I say. "Everything'll be fine."

"I feel so many things, I just feel numb."

It must be genetic.

49

Mary sits on the edge of the front row seat of the Greyhound Bus as it pulls into the Chicago terminal. In the window of the depot she can see a woman with reddish blonde hair and she knows, even without the picture in her hand, she would know: this is her daughter. She walks down the steps of the bus and into Lenore's arms and the two of them stand there, holding tight to each other.

"Hi Mom," says Lenore after a long moment.

"That's all I needed," Grandma tells me later, her voice catching. "Hi Mom!"

They never let go of each other as they walk to a taxi and head for the hotel where they stay up until four in the morning, talking. When they call me at nine a.m. to include me in the fun, they don't sound tired at all. "We wish you were here," Lenore says.

"Hello granddaughter!" Grandma calls in the background.

"We use the same type of words and finish each other's sentences," Lenore continues. "It's just been incredible. We might be eighty and sixty, but I feel like a little kid right now."

"Did you get any sleep at all?" I ask.

"She wants to know if we got any sleep Mom."

Grandma giggles. "Sleep? Who needs sleep?"

"We're still in our pajamas," says Lenore.

"The Atchison, Topeka and the Santa Fe." Grandma is singing. I feel like I've called a sorority after fall rush.

When Grandma gets on the phone, I aim at the profound. "How does it feel to see your daughter after sixty years time?"

"Suffice it to say, it feels rather remarkable."

The two call me daily during their four day reunion. "We've been talking non-stop," Grandma says, "and never seem to run out of things to say."

"We speak so openly about everything," says Lenore. "It doesn't feel like we're strangers at all, but close friends who just lost touch with each other."

"Isn't life delicious!" says Grandma.

"Yes," I agree. And when my grandmother says she's going to visit me in Maryland, I let out a whoop.

This reunion is so different than mine with Lenore. It doesn't seem sacrilegious to have another grandmother. It feels perfect and natural. Yet my comfort with Mary demands that I examine anew the arms-length relationship I have with the woman who gave birth to me, the other mother I have never fully embraced. My grandmother forces me to see how I have held my adoptive family in one hand, like a ball of blue clay, and my birth family in another, like a ball of red, interpreting them as unrelated parts of myself. But they are not separate. They are the same. They belong together. Grandma reshapes my view of my family. She helps me make purple.

The last day of their reunion is Mother's Day, and Mary and Lenore attend Mass together at the cathedral in Chicago. That same morning, Tiff and Jonathon give me a kite, the first one I have owned in thirty years.

The last week my father was alive, we built a kite together. It was a store-bought variety, made of thin wood strips and a plastic cover and cheap string, all for a dime. The face design was a black and white drawing of a rocket blasting off, and I thought, like John Glenn, my kite was going to go up into space.

Dad never saw it fly. He died six days later, and I could never bring myself to take it out into the wind, to race with it in the field off La Cañada Road. Then one day Frankie took it without asking and impaled it on a tree branch. I found it in the trash, the plastic fabric torn, the struts snapped, and I never owned a kite again. Until now.

I run on the hard-packed sand of the beach in Ocean City, Maryland and the kite immediately takes off. This is a much better kite than the dime-store variety. Made of strong colorful nylon with a spinning tail, it soars straight up into the air, as if it knows exactly what it's supposed to do. I hand the string to Tiff, and he lets out more line, and the kite looks smaller and smaller above us. We lie back on the sand and Jonathon takes over. "Cool," he says, as he pulls on the string and the kite dances a hundred feet high in the sky.

I think about my father. What would he think about the fact that I am about to meet my grandmother? How would he feel about the way I have accepted Mary into my heart when I wouldn't eat any of his own mother's polenta? And how would he feel about the letter I plan to write Lenore?

I wish my parents were here. Yet, as I watch the kite in the clouds, with my sons giggling at my side, I sense they are, in fact, with us on this beach.

That night, I write the letter. It is long overdue.

Dear Lenore,

I find myself thinking of you, and of our relationship, and all that has happened... I feel many things at this intersection... The search for Mary was indirectly the search for us, and what we mean to each other. I want you to know - I love you very much.

Your daughter,   Jean

50

Her eyes are blue.

This is the first thing I notice about my grandmother: we have the same eyes. She steps from the jetway and I look into my own face four decades from now. She's five feet tall and when I put my arm around her, we just fit.

We sit with our hands wrapped around mugs of coffee, talking for hours on end. "It *was* a shock when I received Lenore's first letter," Grandma says. "Despite all the reunion stories in the news, I never expected to hear from her, ever. My biggest concern was that I never wanted to hurt her again. My mother feelings surged to the top. I needed to respond to her. I didn't spend much time thinking about what I would say, just wrote down my feelings, put a stamp on the envelope and sat back and waited. And prayed.

"I was so excited when she wrote me back. The first time we talked on the phone, my first thought when the call was over was, 'What a delight!' I almost called her right back."

Our conversations drift from the present to the past. Grandma talks about her time in the Army in World War Two, about the German attack on the island where she was stationed, about her beach landing in France, and the time when her hero, Eleanor Roosevelt, visited the hospital where she was working. "I wish we could have sat down and had a good long talk."

I play an old game, asking, "If you could talk to only one person who is no longer alive Grandma, is Eleanore Roosevelt who you'd choose?"

There is a long pause, then Grandma says softly, "If I could talk to just one person who is no longer alive, it would be my mother. It would mean everything to me just to hear her voice." She stares out the window. "There are so many things I do not understand." She shakes her head. "I believe it all started when my brother died."

"You had a brother?"

She nods. "An older brother, Edwin, born the year before me. He was named after our great grandfather who was killed in the Civil War. I was two months old when it happened, asleep in the baby carriage under the kitchen window of our home in Fond du Lac.

"Mother lit the fire in our old fashioned wood stove, then went to the cellar for more wood. Edwin was just fifteen months old. He opened the drop down door to the stove, took out some burning paper and somehow caught the curtains of the kitchen window on fire. Pieces of the drapes fell with my carriage right there underneath them, but somehow they missed me and landed on my brother instead.

"Mother heard him scream. She raced upstairs to find him on fire and picked him up, rushing out to the cistern where she pumped water on him, dousing the flames. The doctor was summoned, and he placed Edwin in a bathtub full of salt water, which was the best thing they could have done at the time. But they couldn't save him.

Grandma frowns, peeling back the layers, not just for me, but for herself. "I believe his death set everything else in motion. Mother castigated herself over and over, but my father never forgave her. I can only imagine the guilt, the accusations. There was another child, my sister Thelma, but there never was another son.

"Dad moved us bag and baggage from Fond du Lac to Washington State where he got construction work on the railroad. My first memories are from our days along the Columbia River. I caught heck often. One day, I must have been about four, I wasn't supposed to go near the water, and I fell off a dock. I remember dog-paddling furiously until I could stand up, and when I got home, soaking wet, I got a spanking.

"Another time, I was being punished, I don't recall what for, but Mother took Thelma to the silent movies without me. Well, I knew where Mother hid her money. I took a dime and walked to town and bought myself a big bag of butterscotch balls and I ate each and every one. Of course, I got spanked for it, but oh, that butterscotch was good." She grins at the memory.

"When I was eight, Mother moved us to Portland, to a single room in a boarding house. My parents' marriage must have been falling apart, because I have no memory of Dad ever being there. Another man lived with us. He had epileptic seizures and I remember my mother caring for him. What relationship my mother had with this man beyond that, I don't know, but my father came to the door one day and he was angry. That's all I can remember.

"Dad took me away. He left Thelma with Mother and took me all the way back to Fond du Lac. It would be a long time before I would see my mother and sister again.

"I was deposited at his sister Nora's house. Aunt Nora was married to a bootlegger. Uncle John manufactured hootch in the basement, and you could hear him roll the drums of liquor back and forth on the basement floor to age the whiskey.

"Aunt Nora was a devout Catholic and from the moment I arrived, she set about indoctrinating me. She took me to Church and registered me in St. Mary's School. Suddenly, my life had a structure to it. The Church gave me faith and also hope that everything was going to be all right. Well, everything wasn't going to be all right, but the solace I received saw me through my darkest times. Becoming a Catholic changed me completely. I even changed my name. I was born Violet Ellen and that's why you and Lenore had so much trouble finding me. All my legal documents are in that name. But at Aunt Nora's house, I reinvented myself. I became Mary Frances, and that's who I've been ever since.

"A year and a half later, Dad returned, and the next thing I knew I was on a train back to Oregon. I saw my sister, but I was not allowed to see my mother. She had tuberculosis and was in a sanitarium. Thelma and I could only talk to Mother through a window.

"Dad put Thelma and me into a children's home. It was lonely there. I remember that Christmas, feeling so alone. Then a big box of presents arrived from Aunt Nora. I'll never forget that.

"Dad came and got us in February. Mother was dying. I wanted my faith, my strength, to be hers, and I prayed for her to take instruction. This was my mother's gift to me. She asked to receive the sacraments of the Catholic Church.

"I was allowed into the hospital, but I couldn't kiss her. All I could do was cling to end of her metal bed and watch as a priest baptized her and gave her first communion while I silently prayed, 'Don't die yet, Mom, please don't die yet.' And she didn't. She lived through that day, and the next. And then she died.

"My father took us to the funeral home and there was Mother lying on a couch with this shroud wrapped around her. All I could see was her face. Dad left Thelma and me in that room while he made the funeral arrangements. It seemed he was gone an eternity, though it was probably fifteen minutes. I was eleven and I sat with my arm around eight-year-old Thelma in that parlor with our mother's body. I was so frightened. It looked like her eyes were going to pop open any minute. After that, I never slept on my back again, ever. It reminded me too much of my mother at death.

"I never saw my mother's face again. I had no picture of her." Grandma smiles. "Until now." In a cousin's photo album, Lenore had discovered a black and white photograph of Flora standing shyly in a summer dress, her eyes downcast. For the first time in seventy years, Mary is able to see her mother's face. "I'd only had a vague image of her and suddenly, after all these years, I can *see* her." She shakes her head. "So often I wished I had my mother to talk to, but she was gone, her advice lost to me. I learned to survive without her. I let her fade.

"Now, here I am, eighty, and free to re-embrace my own mother. I am able to think about her again, to reflect on her, but there is still so much that I don't know." It is time for another search, but now, instead of one searcher, there are three of us. This time we are looking for someone who is no longer alive: Flora Powers Brown.

51

I sit in the Old Ebbitt Grille, a block from the White House, with my grandmother across the table from me, her face illuminated by evening candle light. There is more of her story I want to hear, more questions I need to ask. "What happened after your mother died?"

"My father took us to Christie Home, an orphanage for girls. Thelma and I were separated because we were three years apart in age, so I rarely saw my little sister after that. It was like I lost my whole family, my mother, my father, and my sister. Even though two of them were still in this world, I had lost them.

"I don't know why my father chose to do this rather than take us back to Fond du Lac where there was family. Not only was Aunt Nora still alive, but so was my grandmother and my mother's brothers and sisters. Did he hate me because I survived and my brother died? Did I remind him too much of my mother? I just don't know.

"I would see him every so often. My father was a carpenter, like his own father, and one of my favorite childhood memories is when he was hired to put in a wood ceiling in the laundry building of the orphanage. He let me get up on the scaffolding with him and nail in the tongue-and-groove boards. I was so proud when it was done.

"There was little abundance at Christie Home. At Christmas, we were permitted to ask for one gift and I asked for some pink cloth to make my sister a dress. She was so surprised on Christmas Day."

"You didn't ask for anything for yourself?"

"There wasn't really anything I needed." Grandma pauses. "Actually, I could have used a few prayers now and again. I still caught heck on occasion and my punishment was always to wax the wooden floor of the main hall. I'd take off the old wax with gasoline, then get down on my hands and knees and rub the new wax into the wood. That hallway seemed a block long to me. I think I spent more time polishing that floor than I ever did in a classroom. Maybe that's why I'm such a good Catholic. I spent my early years on my knees.

"When I was old enough for high school, I was sent to a Catholic school in Portland, where I lived on campus, earning my room and board by washing floors and linens and dishes. I received top honors in my class, earning a scholarship to Marylhurst College, but it covered tuition only and I couldn't afford the books or room and board, so I moved temporarily into my father's boarding house until I found a job.

"That's where it happened. Dad had a girlfriend, Mia, a German immigrant, who lived there with her son, Georg. He was eighteen, just like me, and had the most wonderful smile.

"I was starved for affection I suppose. Most certainly, I was naive. No one ever explained the facts of life to me. I'd never been out on a date or even been around men.

"Something happened between that boy and me in the attic of that boarding house. I don't like to think about it. By the time I learned I was in a family way, I'd gotten a job as a maid and didn't live with my father any longer.

"I went to Florence Crittendon Home and worked for my keep until I delivered your mother. I named her Lenora, after my Aunt Nora. The nuns said I had to have a saint's name in there, so I gave her the middle name of Cecilia because I thought it sounded pretty. It's funny, isn't it, that she became a musician and just by chance I named her after the patron saint of music.

"I took care of her for three wonderful months. The nuns were very supportive, encouraging me to consider adoption. I always felt it was my choice.

"The day I took Lenora to St. Agnes Home was very painful. I was told I would never see my daughter again, and as soon as I walked away, I knew I had to see her again, just one more time. I called and called the Home and finally, they gave me permission. I held her, hugging her close, trying to make up for all the times I wouldn't be able to hold her in the future. I wanted her to know I loved her so very much. Then I had to find the courage to go. I remember closing the door to St. Agnes. It was not easy to walk away. I knew I would never see her again. Hopefully, her life would be a good one. And we would see what would happen with mine.

"I couldn't go back to my father's house. He had married Mia, so Georg's mother was now my step-mother.

"I had nowhere to go. How would I survive? The nuns gave me the path. They helped me to become a nurse.

"This was all a very long time ago," my grandmother says, the light from the Old Ebbitt candle illuminating her eyes, aquamarine. She reaches out and squeezes my hand. "And now, Granddaughter, we are here."

52

Grandma plays Monopoly with the boys at the breakfast table. "Let's see Jonathon, you've landed on Park Place. I have one hotel and two houses. You owe me big bucks." She tests Tiff on the names of all fifty states and their capitols. "Can you spell Montpelier?" She visits Jonathon's first grade class and tells them stories about World War Two.

It is as if she has been a part of our family all along, and all too soon, she returns to her son's home to Illinois. I go into the guest room where she has slept for eight nights and lie back on the big empty bed. My grandmother filled our home with stories and laughter and now the house seems incomplete. I call her to say, "We're missing you back here."

"That's nice to hear." She sounds tired.

"Are you okay?"

"I've got a little infection. The doctor gave me some antibiotics. It's nothing."

I tell her I'll call the following week.

"I love you very much," says my grandmother.

"I love you too."

The next day, Jonathon asks, "Can we go swimming?"

We get into our suits and I'm backing the car out of the driveway, when I hit the brakes and jump out of the car.

"Why are we stopping?" asks Tiff.

"I need to call Grandma." I don't know why I feel a sudden compulsion to do so, but I run into the kitchen and dial.

"Hello?" Her voice is weak and shaky.

"Grandma? What's wrong?"

"I'm not feeling well." She sounds like she's freezing cold.

"Can Bill take you to the doctor?"

"No one's home," she says. "Everyone's out of town."

My mind is races. I don't know anyone in her small town in Illinois. "Let me call a taxi for you." But neither taxi company I reach can get to her in less than an hour, so I do something I know former Army captain and chief surgical nurse Mary Brown will not approve of: I call the police. "My grandmother sounds very ill and I live in Maryland and can't get to her," I tell the dispatcher. "Can you send someone to her house?"

"I'll have an ambulance sent right away. What's her address?"

"Hang on," I say, thumbing through my address book. "I've only known her for a few weeks."

"What?"

"It's a long story. Look, here's her address. Can you please send someone as soon as possible?"

The dispatcher promises she will and I call Grandma back to confess what I've done. She doesn't seem angry, her voice soft, even a little confused. Then she gasps. "I hurt." And the line goes dead.

"No!" We have only just met. This can't be happening.

Tiff stands in the doorway. "Aren't we going to the pool?"

"No!" I shout, but I am not talking to him.

Cheap remote phones. If you dial them too fast they do not keep up. All you hear is silence. I redial. Slower, slow down, it is all going slow now, too slow. I reach the police dispatcher. "She collapsed, my grandmother has collapsed."

"The ambulance is there," the dispatcher tells me. "The paramedic is knocking on her door." A long pause follows.

I hold my breath, standing in my swimsuit on a steamy afternoon in Maryland, while my grandmother with the familiar blue eyes is lying on a floor in Illinois. Did we find her only to lose her? No! I refuse to lose my grandmother so soon.

"She's conscious." The dispatcher's voice filters through my fears. I exhale. How much time has elapsed? A minute? Ten?

Grandma has a fever of almost a hundred and five, a kidney infection and pneumonia, but the doctor at the hospital is optimistic. "It's still early," he says, "but I think she's going to be just fine."

And she is.

She calls me herself the next day, her voice weak but determined. "I'll see you in Fond du Lac next month."

"You sure you'll be up for traveling?"

"Absolutely." She is one unsinkable grandmother, Captain Mary Frances Brown.

53

I have no map, but all the signs on the Wisconsin highway tell me I'm on the correct path.

Pilgrim Way (The Howlands are helping)
Highway 41 (I am 41).
WWII Veterans Memorial Highway (For Captain Mary Brown)
Brownsville (Edwin et. al.)

Cornfields line both sides of the road, tall and green, stretching as far as I can see. It is a hot July day, and it was on a hot July day in 1861 when Edwin marched away from Fond du Lac, never to return. I think about the cornfield in Antietam.

"We'll meet at the white-sided motel right off Highway 41," says Lenore. "I think it's a Day's Inn." Her directions seem rather ambiguous, but there it is, and I pull off on the exit ramp. I can hear giggling when I knock on the door. It swings open and there they are, my birth mother and grandmother, and we laugh in the hallway, locked in an embrace, the three of us together for the first time in our lives.

We buy Fond du Lac sweatshirts and take our picture on the shore of Lake Winnebago. At dinner, Grandma raises her water glass. "To the triumvirate!"

"The triumvirate," Lenore and I echo. We establish Fond du Lac as our national headquarters and agree we'll have annual meetings at the lighthouse on the edge of the lake.

"Grandma's the CEO," I say, "and Lenore, you're the CFO."

"Now wait a minute," says Lenore. "I've never been very good at math."

"All you need is a credit card," I say, handing her the bill for dinner.

"I get it," she grins. "And what, may I ask, are you?"

"I'm the lackey."

"Well, I like that," says Grandma, handing me her coat. "Hang this up for me."

"Yes sir," I salute.

The search for Flora has brought us to this city of our ancestors, and the next morning we descend upon the county records office to see what we can learn about Grandma's mother.

"Jean, look at this." Grandma and Lenore are hunched over an enormous red-leather book of records, Grandma pointing to the middle of the page. "My parents' marriage record."

"January 6, 1915," says Lenore.

"Oh my," says Grandma. The record tells her something she never knew: her parents were married only six months before her brother Edwin was born.

"They had to get married," says Lenore.

"Well, that explains a lot, doesn't it," says Grandma.

We look in other books, at birth and death records. We discover that Flora was the youngest of nine children in the Powers family, and that she was twenty-five years younger than her oldest sibling. "You know," I say, "it's possible that Flora was the illegitimate child of one of the older children in her family, or maybe even adopted, like Lenore and me."

We explore the birth records from the early 1890's to see if we can learn the truth, but find no listing of Flora's birth. I laugh. "She's invisible, just like you, Grandma."

"Must be genetic," Grandma says.

The records clerk is very helpful until I mention that we are trying, in part, to figure out whether or not Flora was adopted. The clerk stiffens. "Those records are sealed." Lenore and I share a look. Been here, done this, too many times, only this time it's laughable. We're trying to find out if someone was adopted a hundred and three years ago and this clerk is worried about maintaining secrecy. Unbelievable.

"I don't think she was adopted," says Grandma after the clerk leaves.

"But Grandma, your mother was ten years younger than her closest sibling."

"Wasn't your mom, Betty, ten years younger than her nearest sister?"

"Well, yes, but her mom was only forty. Your grandmother was close to fifty when Flora was born."

Grandma's jaw is set and I can tell, she doesn't want her mother to be adopted, too, she doesn't want this pattern to go back in time.

"We'll probably never know," says Lenore.

"You're right," I say after hours at the records office and we find nothing to refute or support my theory.

A few miles outside town is the farm where Flora was raised. Grandma has never been to this land before, and she scans the green fields now, as if trying to find her mother. "What a beautiful place," she says. "It's nice to imagine her growing up here."

I think about Flora when she was a young mother, living far from here in Portland, haunted by the ghost of her son, distressed by the separation from the daughter her husband took away, and of her last days, alone in a tuberculosis sanitarium. Memories of these green fields must have seemed like heaven to her.

At nearby Rienzi Cemetery, we try to locate the grave of Edwin Arnold Brown. Long ago, his remains were moved from the tiny family cemetery on Ruth's parents' farm when it was decided that only Piers could be buried there. Ruth bought plots in Rienzi, one for Edwin and one for herself. His lead casket was exhumed, and as it was lifted onto a wagon, the sides collapsed. The men moving the casket looked inside, and they found Edwin's service revolver tucked in his battle sash, still loaded.

Rienzi is enormous. We look and look, but can't find him. Then we spot a grave digger. "Excuse me, we're trying to find the grave of a man named Edwin Arnold Brown."

The grave digger stops and stares at us. "I'm burying a Brown right now."

It turns out it's no relation, but we pay our sincere respects anyway. "This Brown fought in the Civil War," says Grandma.

"Then he'd be in the older part of the cemetery, up there." The grave digger points us toward a grassy knoll covered with trees, and we find Edwin, alongside Ruth and their children, Hattie and Pier. The whole family is at rest in this place.

That evening, the three of us have dinner at a restaurant on the edge of Lake Winnebago, and afterward stand on the shore and watch the sun set. I step away from Lenore and Grandma and take their photograph as they look out over the water. Gold light from the setting sun shines on their faces and I have a flash of my father's face glowing in a similar light, my first memory, so long ago.

What would my parents think of all that has happened, all that I have learned? They are with me here on the shore of this lake in Fond du Lac. They are with me, always.

54

Can the death of a person affect the course of a family for generations?

It is spring, and the blossoms at Antietam Battlefield, white and pink, make the land where Edwin Arnold Brown died less mournful. As Grandma and Lenore and I walk slowly across the empty field beside the Miller farmhouse, I wonder: if Edwin had lived, what would have been different? Would I even have been born? Would Lenore?

Our ancestor's death tore his family asunder. His parents left Fond du Lac after the war, never to return. His father, Isaac, had been mayor of the city, a Wisconsin State Senator, an architect and builder of the unique Octagon House which still stands on Linden Street today. Why did he and Lydia leave such deep roots to move to a remote farm in Delaware?

I cannot ask them. But I know they had lost their only child, a highly esteemed young man described by others as a "universal favorite...admired by all who knew him...who gave himself to his country from the purest patriotism...who, had he lived, had talents which would have carried him to the head of his profession", the law. Were the memories of Edwin too painful for Isaac and Lydia to remain in Fond du Lac?

A collector in northern Maryland owns many of Edwin's letters, as well as the sword he carried into battle. This man has no family connection, but reveres our ancestor's memory, opening his home to Lenore and Grandma and me, letting us read Edwin's letters aloud to each other.

The sword, a gift to Edwin from his men, is heavy in our hands. Its handle is made of ornately carved bronze, and as I run my fingers over the place where his name is engraved, I cannot help wondering, what if? What if he'd survived the war and returned home?

When Edwin died, his family became a ship without a captain, bereaved and broken. Late in life, Ruth told her friends, "I never could get over the shock. I never was my real self again." Emotionally devastated, with no financial resources to sustain her, Ruth split the children up, Hattie remaining with her in Fond du Lac while Louie and Pier went to live in Delaware on Isaac and Lydia's farm.

Louie, the oldest, was the mirror image of his father. Hardworking and scholarly, his grandparents adored him, but they apparently did not adore Pier, Edwin's second son. A letter to Ruth from her own father hints at this.

> *If Father Brown thinks (Pier) is a Burden and Mother Brown feels as though she would rather not have him... I should not wish to have him feel that he must stay where he was not wanted or where his empty room was far preferable to his company...*

When Louie died tragically at seventeen, fourteen-year-old Pier was left with impossible shoes to fill. What kind of man would he grow up to be, what kind of father, without the role model of his own to follow?

When Pier was a grown man of forty, his mother wrote him a letter, her words suggesting that weakness and insecurity plagued him as an adult, and indicating her own regrets as a single parent.

> *My dear boy. I wish you were independent so you would not have to have your feelings hurt so often... I wish I had had the knowledge when you were young and reasoned with you instead of using the rod. You might have been better fitted to bring up your children...*

What would Pier's life have been like if his father had survived Antietam and the war? Would he have been a different man with his father's influence? Was his destiny shaped by personality or circumstance? Answers are beyond my grasp, for, as Edwin's own best friend, Rufus Dawes, once wrote, his "voice is forever silent."

Yet Dawes' own fate makes for an interesting comparison. He and Edwin shared much in common. They were officers of similar temperaments, near each other in age, college educated with ambitions to lead good and productive lives, Edwin as a lawyer, Rufus as a businessman.

Rufus Dawes did not die in the Civil War. He served in the Sixth Wisconsin, throughout, most notably on the first day of Gettysburg, when he led the men of the Iron Brigade against Confederate troops, holding their own until the rest of the Union Army could arrive. When he mustered out in 1865, Dawes was a Brigadier General, and a true hero. He married his wartime sweetheart, and together, they raised four sons. He had a successful business career, even serving for a term in Congress before his death.

While visiting Madison, Wisconsin, with Jon for his college reunion, I stop by the State Historical Society and discover Rufus Dawes's personal diaries in their collection. It is a moving experience to hold this man's small leather-bound journal and to read his handwritten accounts of Antietam and of Edwin.

Two days later, back home in California, Tiff asks if I will drive him to the used bookstore in our village. While he browses the shelves, I walk through the shop and a single title catches my eye: The Portrait of an American. Pulling the book from the shelf, I glance at its jacket, and see it is a biography of a man named Charles Dawes. Could he be related to Rufus?

My question is answered on the very first page. Charles was the oldest son of Rufus Dawes. I leave the shop with the old book tucked under my arm and read about Charles late into the night.

Charles Dawes led a good life, a life strongly influenced by his father. His childhood was stable and full of opportunity.

Pier Brown, Edwin's son, was raised in a fatherless home by a mother who never fully recovered from the loss of her husband. Ruth's obituary stated, "The horrors of war had much to do with shaping the destiny of Mrs. Ruth Brown..." No doubt, those same horrors shaped her son, Pier, ultimately impacting *his* children, as well. Pier's son, my great grandfather, Ed, chose to put his daughter Mary in an orphanage rather than return her to his family in

Fond du Lac. Why? Are events of my grandmother's childhood related to a bullet at Antietam?

I'd like to think that Edwin's children would have had better lives if he'd lived, lives similar to the ones Rufus Dawes was able to provide for his children.

Can the loss of one person affect a family for generations? I believe it can. When four-year-old Pier Brown watched his father's coffin lowered into the ground, his future sank with it. He never went to college. Before his father's death, he was described as "the most industrious child you'd ever see, a philosopher." Such traits were no longer evident in the adult Pier Brown, who lived in the shadow of his dead brother and father.

Unlike Pier, Charles Dawes was raised in a home that was not destroyed by war. He followed in his father's footsteps, attending college and becoming a successful businessman.

In 1924, he was elected Vice President of the United States and won the Nobel Peace Prize.

55

Destiny is born of random events.

We are moving again, this time to a college in California. As I pack up the books and files in my office, I come across a carton unopened since our last move. I glance at the magic marker label, "Mom's Desk", and cut the tape, thinking it is stuff from my roll-top. It is not.

Ten years ago when she died, I filled this box with my mother's things from her maple desk in the living room. I glance at the assortment of junk and smile. Mom used to complain I was a pack rat, but she was no different. There are postcards from the 1939 World's Fair, matchbooks and swizzle sticks from restaurants in the 1940's where she and Dad went on dates, discharge papers from the Army, calendars, notecards and other mementoes from four decades, and near the bottom is something I haven't seen since I was twelve: the Wenger family tree.

Long ago, when I had seen the word (adopted) under my name, I had felt excluded, as if my membership in my mother's family had to be explained. But now that I have my own family tree, the word seems less exclusive. I sit on the floor of my office and read about my mother's family for the first time.

They were German-Swiss. During the summer when I was twenty, Mom and I had traveled to Wengen, Switzerland, the fairy tale village from which her ancestors emigrated. Perched on a shelf overlooking the Interlaken Valley, Wengen was shrouded in fog. We took a ski tram up through the clouds and the surrounding Alps awaiting us in the sunlight above took our breath away.

"That's Wenger Alp," the tram operator told us, pointing at a small triangular peak in the distance.

"That was named for my family," Mom says. I take a picture of her standing proudly in front of it and don't point out that she didn't say *our* family. It didn't make me feel bad. It made me feel good to see her so excited.

As I read the family tree, I learn that Mom's grandmother, Sophie Bookmiller, was eight-years-old when her family left Wengen in 1856 to travel to Pennsylvania. Tragedy struck. Sophie's mother died on the voyage and was buried at sea. Shortly thereafter, her father remarried, and his new wife didn't want the burden of his three children, so Sophie, along with her brother and sister, were placed in separate foster homes.

Adoption is part of my mother's family history! I wonder if Mom ever read this family tree after she buried it in the drawer long ago, if she knew that her grandmother grew up in an adoptive home.

Sophie married a minister, moved to Ohio and raised seven children. Her oldest daughter, Effie, had seven children of her own, the youngest of whom was my mother.

Sophia Bookmiller	John Brumbaugh	Mary Ann Baker	William Wenger
b. 1848	b. 1848	b. 1858	b. 1851
seven children	d. 1932	d. 1924	

	Effie Brumbaugh	Stanley Wenger	
	b. August 21, 1880	b. May 8, 1879	
	d. August 30, 1948	d. August 28, 1972	

Infant son	Arden	Ruth	Bernice	Martha	Dorothy	Betty Lou Wenger
b. 1901	b.1903	b.1904	b.1906	b.1910	b.1911	b. 2/1/1921
d. 1901	d.1917	d. 1993	d. 1999		d. 1992	d. 2/15/1987

I am enchanted by Sophie's story, and feel a kinship with her, a fellow adoptee. She helps me see how chance plays a role in family history, for if her mother had survived the voyage to America, Sophie might never have met John Brumbaugh and my mother might never have been born to adopt me.

My parents were able to meet because of Sophie's fate, and because of something that happened in 1892. I became their child, in part, because of a cask of wine.

Baldesare Sacconaghi, my dad's grandfather, was born in the small village of Lonate Pozzolo in northern Italy. Married to Antonia Regalia, mother of their four children, he worked as the caretaker at an estate belonging to a wealthy family.

One day, the owner of the estate was down in the cellar when a barrel of wine exploded. Baldesare heard the sound and rushed over to find his

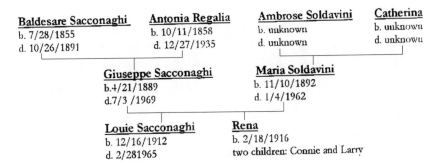

employer on the cellar steps, drenched in wine. Baldesare thought it was blood, had a seizure, and died. He was thirty-six.

There was no life insurance, nothing, and Antonia was left alone to raise four children, the youngest of whom, Giuseppe, my grandfather, was only two. When he was fifteen, my grandfather came to America to seek his fortune, ultimately settling in Santa Barbara, California. He worked hard, and by the time he was twenty-one, had made enough money to settle down. A marriage was arranged back in Italy and eighteen-year-old Maria Soldavini made the long journey to southern California by boat and train.

The American Dream belonged to them. They saved enough money to buy a house, a car, and had two children, Luigi and Rena.

Luigi, my dad, changed his name to Louie, and like his father before him, worked hard. He was quarterback of the football team at Santa Barbara High, star of the senior play, president of the student welfare council, and made the honor roll every semester. Under his name in the yearbook are the words "our noblest and most valorous." Two hundred friends signed his annual.

Louie,

I know you are going a long way with few advantages. You are a hard worker, a good student, good athlete, and a friend worth having and keeping.

Here's to a fellow with everything that will make success - bearing, guts and personality.

He went on to graduate from Cal Berkeley, then entered the Army where he became a captain in the 11ᵗʰ Calvary. As the United States entered World War Two, my father was sitting on top of a horse. His commanding general believed that calvary units would be effective in night combat against German Panzer tanks. But before Dad was ever sent overseas to fight a tank from the back of a horse, it was discovered he had diabetes, and the Army reassigned him to the finance office in Oakland, California.

His Army scrapbook contains a picture of him astride a sawhorse in his regulation Calvary hat and nineteenth-century lace-up boots. There are also photos of several women. He was thirty-three, a bachelor, and there was Dina at Lake Tahoe and Gyrt at Tilden Park and Joyce and Elsie at the beach. The pictures end when he met my mom. They married shortly after VE-Day, and after several childless years of marriage, they adopted Frankie, and then, a year and a half later, they adopted me.

All because Sophie's mother died at sea and because Giuseppe's father died when a cask of wine exploded.

Destiny is born of random events, like an accidental death or a decision to move - or which couple an adoption agency chooses to raise a child.

56

A friend from Lafayette calls. "I thought you should know. Frankie came by our house yesterday, asking for money."

I haven't seen or corresponded with my brother for years. I wasn't even sure he was still alive. "Did you give him any?" I ask.

"Just a few dollars."

"I'm sorry. I'll reimburse you."

"It's not that." I can tell his visit left her nervous. "We just thought you should know."

The last time I saw Frank was at Mom's funeral. How will I reach him? I call the county to see if he still has a conservator. He does. The conservator in turn gives me the number of Frank's psychiatrist.

"My brother is one of your patients, and I'm concerned that he's traveling all the way out to our old neighborhood looking for money. Is he okay?"

"I haven't noticed anything unusual," says the psychiatrist.

"Can you have him call me collect?"

"Of course."

What's he like now? How could I have let so much time go by without contacting him?

"You have a collect call from Frank," says the operator.

"I'll accept," I say quickly. "Frankie?"

"What the f___ do you want?" says my brother. And I remember why he's out of my life. I wouldn't lock him out. But after ten years, that's all he can say.

Mom told me when she was dying, "I don't want you to take on this burden." It had been an easy promise for me to make. He is not a part of my life. Would it make a difference if he were? Would it help him if I took an active interest in his needs? Did Mom make a difference? Yes. I know she did.

I watch the home movies again, of Frankie and me dancing for Grandma and Grandpa, of us riding ponies around a ring in Santa Barbara, of us tearing open packages at Christmas. In the most precious clip, we stand beside Dad, one of the only moments our father was ever on film, kneeling between us, laughing. At the last moment, Dad leans over and kisses me on the cheek and I wrap my arms around his neck.

Frankie was there for all of it. He is the touchstone for my early childhood, and I am his.

He wore a suit to Mom's funeral. He did not write anything on his forehead. He sat with the rest of us in the little cabin on the Neptune Society boat, waiting for our turn up on deck, his knee bouncing up and down nervously.

The boat circled around Angel Island and the minister came and got us, said a few words, and then I spread our mother's ashes in San Francisco Bay, as she'd asked me to do. I offered Frankie the chance to help me perform this rite, but he declined.

Earlier that week, I'd driven Mom's car over to the hotel where Frankie was living, and together we carried her television set and some of her furniture and cartons of mementos up to his room. I opened a box and took out a framed photo of Mom and Dad and put it on the coffee table.

"Do you have any money on you?" Frank asked.

I gave him a hundred dollars.

He asked again as we got off the Neptune Society boat. "Do you have any cash? I need some money."

I gave him all I had. He frowned. "This is it?"

I nodded and turned away. I did not watch him leave. I did not wave goodbye. I did not have anything more to say.

I am a griot, yet I have turned away from my own brother. Family. Sometimes it is not easy at all.

57

Grandma has never been here before. We walk slowly into the marble mausoleum at the Hollywood Cemetery, Grandma holding onto my arm, her face painted with the colored light of stained glass windows, the smell of burning candles in the air. I know where to find the plaque on the wall.

Edwin A. Brown
1892-1962

I leave my grandmother with her father's remains.

"How do you feel?" I ask later as we sit beside the duck pond near Douglas Fairbank's memorial.

She pulls her knees up under her chin, looking like a young girl. "I was living in New Jersey, married, with children, when I got the letter from Mia telling me my father had died. That was it. He was gone. Why wasn't I invited to his funeral?" She is not asking me this. "There are some things I will never understand, and I can never talk to him about them." She looks away, across the water.

A mile away is the address where her father and Mia were living the year he died. There are no longer any apartment buildings on the Los Angeles block, only an empty lot and a strip mall with signs all in Korean. "I can't picture my father here," Grandma says. "It must have looked different forty years ago."

In Marina Del Rey, we walk out the long pier, find an empty bench, and sit without words, looking at the Pacific surf. I put my arm around her shoulders and we watch the seagulls hovering above the fishermen and the pelicans playing in the curl of the waves. Suddenly, Grandma says, "I'm not afraid of dying."

"Well good," I grin. "You're not going to for a long time."

She looks at me. "Have you thought about what you'll do when I die?"

I stop smiling. "What do you mean?"

"I mean, about your mother."

The waves crash against the pilings beneath us and I avoid Grandma's eyes. "You mean Lenore?"

"Yes. What kind of relationship will you have with her?"

"I don't know." I shift on the hard bench. "I don't want to think about you being gone."

"It's going to happen." Her hand touches mine.

"I'll miss you Grandma."

"It will be hardest on her."

"It will be hard on everyone."

"Jean." I look into her familiar eyes. "I need to know you'll be there for her."

"Okay. Sure."

She shakes her head. "I have a bond with you unlike what I have with anyone else. And what we have between the three of us has given me a reason to want to live more years." Our hands are tightly woven together. "I'm asking you now, because I need to know. When I die, what will you do?"

I cannot lie. "Sometimes it feels like Lenore is my sister. When she talks about you, she always calls you Mom, as if you were my mom too."

"Well I'm not," Grandma says. "Lenore is your mother, just like Betty, and I'm asking you to be there for her when I'm gone."

Her eyes are blue, just like mine. "I will, Grandma. I promise."

We have daily adventures. Jonathon and Tiff teach Grandma how to play Boggle. They quickly regret this. "I have oyster," Grandma says. "Do you have oyster?"

"No." They stare at her long list of words.

"Stoic."

"That's not a word."

"Yes, it is," she says. "Stoop?"

"You win," Jonathon sighs, rattling the letters to play another round.

We paint ceramic mugs one day, buying a frame for her picture of her mother the next, and take the boys on a long walk through the botanical garden. When my cousin Larry joins us for dinner, Grandma serenades him with "Ragtime Cowboy Joe", a capella.

We dine at Chevy's and the waiter gives her a big colorful sombrero even though it isn't her birthday. She is wearing it as she walks across the airport tarmac and up the stairs to her plane, on her way home. She turns and waves to me, then disappears, leaving me feeling empty and full at the same time.

58

I have only one picture of my great-grandmother, Mia. She is middle-aged, seated on a piano bench, her heavy arms folded across her chest, her broad shoulders something a linebacker would envy. She is not smiling.

I do not like Mia. I cast blame upon her before I ever see her unsmiling face in this black and white photo. "She could be very intimidating," people who knew her say. "She pretty much ran things."

Grandma says, "She was very bossy. I didn't like her. She said I should call her 'Mama', but, of course, I wouldn't."

I envision my strong-willed grandmother, confident enough to change her name at the age of nine, tough enough to have survived her mother's death, the orphanage, the loss of her first child to adoption, ambitious enough to earn a college scholarship, to become a nurse and join the Army. I imagine her test of wills with this German housefrau, her father's girlfriend. I can see their collision vividly.

"Georgie was the apple of Mia's eye," an old woman in Portland said. "Her son was her whole life."

Lenore's birth certificate says in the box for father, 'Georg (admitted, later denied).' I see Mia's hand in this denial. I hold her responsible for Grandma having to put Lenore up for adoption.

But Grandma doesn't hold Mia responsible. "I remember the nuns more than anyone else. They helped me, encouraging me make something of myself. My father and Mia aren't part of my memories surrounding Lenore's adoption at all."

Nonetheless, I decide that Mia controlled everyone, including Ed, that she banished Mary from the family simply to protect her beloved Georg. I base my conclusions about her on a handful of anecdotes from people who knew her long ago, and from a single photograph where she doesn't smile. I believe that Mia was a stubborn, self-centered, person. Until the book.

"Mia wrote a book," Lenore says. "Jim Brown's sister has a copy she'll loan us."

"What kind of a book?" I think of Mia's broad shoulders and imagine it has something to do with weight lifting.

"It's called 'How I Escaped the Red Guns'."

"What is it? A novel?"

"No, it has something to do with what happened in Munich after World War One."

Mia's book arrives in the mail. It is short, just a hundred and seventeen pages long. It doesn't tell me everything I want to know, only covering six years, from 1919 to 1925. But it is enough.

"I look for the last time," Mia wrote, "from a hillside above the murmuring Isar stream, among scented flower carpets, surrounded by the Bavarian Alps, at my home..."

Mia was a member of Munich's middle class. Her first husband was a U-Boat commander who was killed in the Atlantic. She married his brother, Richard, a German infantryman, who was badly wounded after two-and-a-half years in the trenches, spending a year in the hospital recovering from his wounds. When the war ended, they lived in a villa that had been in Mia's family for generations, with her mother, and her two little sons, Artur and Georg, as well as her two dogs, Ralph and Prinz, and thirty-one chickens.

The post-war situation in southern Germany was ripe for anarchy. The nation was defeated, the economy a shambles, and in her book, my great grandmother teaches me something I never knew before: similar to the revolution taking place in Russia, Communist Red Guards took over Munich in 1919. Called Spartakists, they preyed upon the middle class, seizing property and terrorizing people. Mia's dogs were poisoned, the flock of chickens, beheaded. And then Mia was arrested.

Held for ransom in a cell with two dozen other people, Mia's crime was being affluent enough to own a silent movie cinema. Richard bought her release, only to have Mia rearrested on her way home from jail.

"More money," the Spartakists told Richard. They grilled Mia. "Tell us about your neighbors. How much money do they have?" When Mia refused to answer, they tortured her, binding her arms upon a table, cutting into her flesh. "Tell us what you know!"

Mia's twenty-three cellmates were treated similarly. There was the college professor, the young student, and the old man who kept wailing, "My wife, my daughter." When Richard paid again for Mia's freedom, she promised to help the others try to gain their release, but all of them were shot, one by one, and buried in a common grave.

When the German government finally suppressed the Spartakists, Mia learned she and Richard had been next on the Red Guard's list for execution. But, although order was restored to Munich, Mia's personal life disintegrated. Pregnant with her third child, she learned Richard was having an affair with a seventeen-year-old girl and wanted a divorce. Then her mother became ill and little Artur came down with high fever. Both died within days of each other. Just three days after Mia buried her oldest son, she miscarried the child within her.

All Mia had left was Georg. The villa was sold and she got a job as an accountant. Inflation was rampant: the apartment she rented in Munich was 24 million marks a month. When a relative in Oregon invited her to come to America, Mia jumped at the chance.

Before she left, she took a wreath of flowers to the mass grave of the hostages with whom she'd shared a cell, and another wreath to the graves of her mother and son. Then she and ten-year-old Georgie boarded the ocean liner *President Harding* and sailed to New York. Mia's book ends there in November of 1925 with a poem.

> *My words shall reach thee, no matter where,*
> *To bring the story which is thine and mine...*

Beneath a Tall Tree ❧ page 233

Her story, of course, didn't end. She settled in Oregon and later, California. Georg grew up to fight as an American GI in World War Two.

"She was very forceful," say people who knew her. "Georgie was her whole life."

It all makes sense now. Mia steps three dimensional from the pages of her own book. I no longer look at the photo and see a broad-shouldered German house Frau. I see my great grandmother's fierce eyes. The set of her jaw. I see *her*.

59

"Auntie Jean!" Twelve-year-old Collin grins as he pushes open the sliding glass door, racing to hug me, followed closely by his brothers, Taylor and Reed. I have known my brother Jim's sons since they were babies, but I was never supposed to know them at all. I was never supposed to have any desire to find anyone from my birth family.

My parents were given a book when they adopted me which stated that, "A child adopted very young has no real picture of his biological parents, and no idea of what they were like... He therefore has no real kinship to them." And if the adoptee should ask about his biological family, the adoptive parents shouldn't mistake such questions as a yearning to know them. "This is false in every case."

False in every case. Who decided that?

Implicit in the language and secrecy of closed adoption were unspoken rules I was to follow:

> *Never wonder about where you came from.*
> *If you ever do, you are betraying the people who love you.*
> *The people in your original family are better off not knowing you.*
> *Never view yourself as important enough to question these rules.*

Despite the best of intentions, the lawmakers and policy makers who shaped adoption in America knew nothing about what it was like to be adopted. They knew nothing about me or my parents or my birth parents and how their imposed secrecy would affect us.

What difference has it made for me that I now know Lenore, and seven brothers and sisters, and thirteen nieces and nephews, and a grandmother with eyes that are blue like mine?

"If you'd never met them," a social worker points out, "you wouldn't be missing anything. How can you miss something you don't know you have?"

But what about how wonderful it feels to have them in my life?

"Admit it," the woman says. "You were just lucky. It could have been a disaster."

Really? Is knowing the truth really a disaster? It's been my observation that reuniting birth family members generally leads to enlightenment, not to catastrophe.

What if I never knew my brother Jim and his sons, Taylor, Collin, and Reed?

"Simple," says this woman. "They wouldn't know. You wouldn't know."

Yeah, but I do know. I *know* what would have been missing. I can close my eyes and see the empty space.

"Auntie Jean!" Collin's arms are wrapped tight around me. This is not an obligatory 'go give your aunt a hug,' this is spontaneous and heartfelt. I have a nephew who loves me.

Actually, I have more than one. I go to watch Collin's younger brother Reed play in a basketball tournament. He is ten, with reddish auburn hair and a great hook shot. His team is number one in the entire state of Minnesota and his mother and I sit on the bench, shouting louder than any of the fathers in the stands.

I was there on the field the first time Reed ever played in a baseball game. Collin's team was short a player, so Reed was put in the lineup. He was six, wearing a pink t-shirt and purple socks as he adjusted his glasses and touched the plate with his bat like a pro. He slugged one out into left field and I took the first snapshot of him rounding the bases, a pink blur with purple ankles, his batting helmet slightly askew, his eyes focused intensely on the base in front of him.

I don't get to see my nephews often. Two thousand miles separate us and months go by without seeing them. One night, while talking with Jim on the phone, I hear Taylor's voice in the background. "Can I say hi?" I get a small dose of my adolescent nephew, his voice cracking, deepening. He is becoming a man, slowly, in fits and starts. The last time I saw him, he had grown past my eye level. He is only fourteen, but I now look up to him.

"Hey Taylor," I say in my wrestle-take-down voice.

"Hi Auntie Jean."

After a few minutes, Jim says, "Come on Tay. This is on her nickel."

"Okay, okay," says Taylor. There is a pause, then he says softly, "I love you Auntie Jean."

Middle-aged auntie tears fill my eyes. "I love you too, Tay."

What difference does it make that I learned the truth, that I know people I was never supposed to know and beat a system designed to protect me?

I just have more people to love, that's all. And that ain't bad.

60

We meet in Oregon in July. It is not an easy trip.

The three of us are the only people in the waiting room at the Salvation Army Home. "Mom, how can you not remember," Lenore says to Mary. "This is where you gave birth to me."

"I'm sorry," Grandma frowns, "but I just don't remember this place."

I sit in an armchair fifteen feet away, but even at this distance I can see the tiny tense lines on Lenore's face. She's upset. She has brought her mother to this place, the very building where she was born, to walk the halls, to relive those lonely days together. Grandma had said at breakfast, "If it will make you feel better to go there, then I will go. But there is no real need."

"Yes there is," Lenore insisted. She is on a mission. She wants to stick it to the people who hurt her, who controlled her life for so long, to thumb her nose at the powers that be and show them she succeeded in breaking through their barriers. I want to say: those people are dead and gone, it's over, it doesn't matter anymore. But it does matter - to her. "I just can't believe you don't remember this," she says sharply to Mary.

I have never heard her angry at her mother before. She is acting like an angry child, bitter and abandoned. I am very uncomfortable.

So is Grandma, but unlike me, she is not retreating to a chair across the room. She stands in front of her daughter and says patiently, "Lenore, I can't tell you what you want to hear because it wouldn't be true. I can't tell you I remember this place, because I don't. But I love you. I would never deny you. That will have to be enough."

Lenore is past reason. "I refuse to believe you can't remember being here!" This is the low point. Right now, right here in this brick building, Lenore is bouncing off the bottom.

Grandma begins to lose patience. "It was over sixty years ago. Maybe they remodeled. Let's go get some coffee and talk about something else."

But Lenore will not let go. I have been where she is. I have been angry without understanding why, and been unable to move past bad feelings. "Yeah, coffee sounds good," I say.

"No!" Lenore snaps, her arms tightly crossed, glaring at us. "We're going to the room where you gave birth to me, Mom."

"Hello." We turn at the woman's voice in the doorway. "I'm the director. I hear you'd like to tour the facility." She looks nice.

"That's right," Lenore says sharply. Nice doesn't work for her right now. This woman, this director, represents the enemy. "I visited here three years ago," Lenore says, "and saw the room where I was born in 1934. This is my mother and I've brought her here to see it."

"But that's impossible," says the director.

"No it's not!" Lenore's voice rises with her anger. "I was allowed to see it three years ago, and I want to show it to my mother. Now."

"You don't understand," says the director. "This facility wasn't built until after you were born. It didn't exist in 1934."

Grandma's face lights up like a Christmas tree. "No wonder I didn't recognize it!"

"But I was told," Lenore stumbles, "three years ago they told me this was it, the place where I was born."

"You were given the wrong information," the woman says gently. "The building where you were born was down in the flatland."

"It can't be."

"They tore it down a long time ago, but I can give you the address."

Grandma is beaming, vindicated. Lenore is like a jammed circuit. She understands the information, but she can't yet erase what she's been led to believe all these years. Beneath her anger and frustration is incredible pain. It is difficult to see her like this, difficult to know the right thing to say. She is a raw, open wound. In silence, we drive down the hill to the address where the home for unwed mothers used to be, the place where Lenore was actually born. "Now, this looks familiar," says Grandma. "I recognize these streets."

"My god," says Lenore. "I used to live just a couple blocks from here." Her waves of anger recede. Next, we drive south, to Christie Home, the orphanage where Grandma and her little sister lived.

Grandma recognizes the three story colonial building the instant we turn in the driveway. "This is it!" Christie Home is now a facility for troubled teens, and a counselor takes us through the living quarters. "This was my room. Twelve of us lived in here," Grandma says. "Good night Miss Agnes, it's barely changed at all."

The counselor leads us down to the ground floor, telling us how the building was used as a set for the deaf school in *Mr. Holland's Opus.*" I recognize the hallway from the movie. But Grandma is remembering something else. She stands in the center of the hardwood corridor, gazing toward the double doors at the other end and suddenly I know. "Grandma, this is it, isn't it? This is *the* hallway."

"Yes."

I always thought Grandma was exaggerating it's size when she described having to wax it, but it does look a block long. "We'd start at one end," Grandma remembers, "strip it with gasoline, apply the wax, and then buff it by hand. It took forever."

We cross the grounds to what had been the orphanage laundry. Today, it houses artisans. There is a kiln, and studios, and upstairs, a crafts store. We wander through, looking at the various items for sale, from scarves to fountains to sculpture. Grandma and Lenore stop in an aisle, staring upward, and I literally trip over them. "What's going on?" Lenore points at the old wainscoting ceiling.

"I built this with my father," says Grandma.

The three of us stand with our heads tilted back, admiring the wood as if it were the Sistine Chapel. Grandma and her father hammered in these boards in 1928, and they are still here today.

We leave Christie Home and continue south, with one last thing to do: find Flora's grave. The cemetery is far down the Interstate. I called the caretaker ahead of time and confirmed that Flora is buried there. "Her name's on our rolls, but not the location of her internment. I have to warn you, a lot of people who died in the sanitarium are buried in unmarked graves."

It is an old cemetery, overgrown and empty of visitors. Grandma thinks she remembers the spot. "It was near the front. I seem to remember this tree." She points at an old oak, squinting, trying to remember the day of her mother's funeral in early March of 1927, three months before Lindbergh crossed the Atlantic. We walk from one end of the cemetery to the other, but do not find a stone for Flora. "The caretaker said not everyone has a marker," I say.

"But she has to have one," says Grandma. "She had a family. She wasn't forgotten."

I continue to walk the grounds until Lenore calls to me. "Come on, Jean, let's go." But I don't want to give up. They wait as I walk the entire place again, peering under bushes along the fence line, looking for a lost stone, a broken stone. But unlike Lydia Arnold Brown's grave marker, I do not find one here in Oregon hidden beneath vines or a layer of soil. We leave knowing that Flora Powers Brown lies beneath the earth with no stone bearing her name.

We drive toward the airport in silence. Of all the journeys we have made together, this one has been the most difficult. "It just doesn't seem right," says Grandma after a long time, "that there's nothing with her name on it anywhere."

Lenore squeezes her hand as Grandma gazes out the window, determined. She nods to herself after a long moment. "I'm going to do something about this."

61

Tiff's godparents have a son, Shane, the same age, and the two boys have always claimed each other as 'godbrothers'. Neither of Jonathon's godparents have children, so he does not have a 'godbrother'. Jealousy erupts. "Shane's my godbrother too," Jonathon says after a visit.

"No he's not." Tiff doesn't want to share his special connection to Shane.

On a vacation with Shane and his parents, along with another couple whose son is also their godson, I find Jonathon sitting alone on the dock. "They're all godbrothers and I'm not," he says.

"They're your friends just like they're Tiff's friends," I say. "It's no different, really."

"Yes it is," insists my eight-year-old son. "Can I have a godbrother?"

"Well, sure," I say, hoping to make him feel better, and at that he smiles and skips away.

Months later we visit Barbara and George and their son Gabriel at their home in the New England countryside. Long ago, Tiff and Jonathon had dyed Gabriel's hair green, and this event gave birth to a friendship, not just between the boys, but between our two families. As Barbara and I drink coffee, watching the boys run through the fields, Jonathon races up out of breath. "Gabriel and I have decided we want to become godbrothers, okay?"

I remember my promise on the dock. When I explain his request, Barbara laughs. "Would turning their hair green be considered an appropriate baptism?"

Ultimately, we nix the hair-dying idea, but giggling, she and I script a ceremony to unite our sons as godbrothers. At the stroke of nine in the evening we request that everyone congregate on the front lawn where we have set up a ring of citronella candles. "You stand in the center," says Barbara to the boys.

I clear my throat. "We are gathered here together to join Jonathon and Gabriel in holy god-brotherhood..." I do not look at Barbara as I say this because if I do, I will burst out laughing. Instead I focus on tall, broad-shouldered Jonathon and small, slender Gabriel, who stare at me as if I am a priest at high mass. "This union we create between our sons is the sacred one that exists between brothers." Barbara and I had snickered when we thought this up, but as I say the words out loud now, my voice catches and it is a moment before I can continue.

"These two boys have known each other almost their entire lives, and it is because of their friendship that our two families remain close, despite the separation of thousands of miles. They are responsible for uniting us all."

A breeze rises from the meadow, making the candles flicker and our shadows dance. I look from the boys, to George and Barbara and Jon, and see the future, when we parents are no longer around. Fighting tears, not laughter, I address our sons. "You know what brothers do for each other?" They nod solemnly. "They're loyal. They never lie to each other. They stand up for each other. They would even die for each other if it ever came to that."

"Wow," Gabriel whispers.

"Do you promise to be there for each other, forever and always?"

They nod.

Barbara steps forward, holding a bowl of ashes she collected from the fireplace, and she smears a black ring upon each boy's forehead. "This symbolizes the circle of life, a journey brothers make together."

"And now, to complete this," Jon says as he steps behind Gabriel.

"We will perform the ancient egg ritual." George grins behind Jonathon. Eggs are a part of our families history together, from Easter Egg hunts to the exchange of red eggs on Greek Orthodox Easter. One morning, our two families even pitted our individual skills against each other in a contest to see who could keep raw eggs from breaking when thrown off Barbara and George's roof. Everyone created their own design, from the kids to the grownups, engineering contraptions that would cushion the eggs, using a wide variety of materials to try to 'win', everything from empty milk cartons filled with cotton to Gabriel's favorite pillow. So it seems appropriate now that eggs be used in the ritual by which our sons become god-brothers.

"This ancient rite is performed by the fathers of the tribe," George says. "You first Jon."

With that, Jon cracks an egg over Gabriel's beautiful blond hair, and George cracks an egg over Jonathon's crew cut. The yolks break and slide in gooey yellow strings down their hair, over their foreheads, down onto their cheeks. The boys murmur, "Gross," simultaneously, but stand stock still.

"And now," says Barbara, "for the ancient cleansing ritual." She and I step forward with a bucket of water, and dowse the boys until they are drenched to the skin, squealing and laughing.

"Okay," I proclaim. "That's it. You're brothers now."

Laughing, the boys stand, soaking wet, with their arms across each other's shoulders, and I realize something has happened, something unexpected. We had done it as a joke, but right there in front of our eyes, our sons became god-brothers. And in becoming brothers, they have made our two families, one.

62

They call him Cheddar Man. He is a 9000 year old skeleton found in a cave near Cheddar, England. Scientists at Oxford University do DNA tests on one of his molars, looking specifically at his mitochondrial DNA, which is virtually unchanged through his maternal line. In this way they determine that Cheddar Man is related to a school teacher living in this tiny English village.

I like that Cheddar Man's maternal DNA can tell us who his family is nine millennia after his death. Women don't exist much in our history. We've always been around, but our contributions weren't encouraged or recorded. Like the DNA in Cheddar Man's tooth, our foremothers have remained hidden and unvalued until very recently.

Ten years ago, there wasn't a single statue honoring women in the nation's capitol. Now Lenore and I follow Grandma into the Memorial to Women in the Military in Washington, D.C.

Mary (Brown) Miklosey: Army Nurse Corps Feb 1941 to Apr 1947. Mary was single and an orphan when she signed up as a Reserve nurse...

The computerized archive cites Grandma's entire military service, from the day she tended sailors injured in a U-Boat attack on Aruba, to the months she spent at Camp Lucky Strike in France helping prepare emaciated U.S. soldiers, freed from German prison camps, for the journey home. The memorial is spectacular, and makes me proud of my grandmother's service to the country. There is much about my grandmother that makes me proud: her kindness, her faith, her enthusiasm to learn, her intelligence and wit, her capacity to love. She is a survivor.

Together, we have journeyed to many places, and spent a great deal of time talking about those who came before us. Lenore and Grandma and I have gotten to the point where we talk about our ancestors as if we are reminiscing about old friends, about people we have actually known.

In late summer, we meet in Fond du Lac at the same hotel we always do, falling into each other's arms, laughing. We are the triumvirate and I am invincible with the two of them in this place.

"Mom," says Lenore at dinner. "Tell Jean what you did today."

Grandma looks at me proudly. "I am a landowner."

"What?"

"She bought a cemetery plot," Lenore explains.

Grandma opens her purse and pulls out the document. "I've decided I want to be buried here in Fond du Lac. I was born here, and I want to return here." There was a single plot left on the gentle slope where Edwin Arnold Brown is buried with his children. Only a descendant of Edwin can be buried there, and it seems most appropriate that this sacred ground now belongs to Mary Frances Brown, the first member of the family to serve as a Captain in the Army since her great grandfather died at that rank at Antietam.

As we drive through the entrance of Rienzi Cemetery, fifty American flags flutter in the wind, a nice touch for the visiting Captain Brown. I like knowing my grandmother will be here beside Edwin and Ruth for all her descendants to find a hundred years from now.

Afterward, we visit our favorite places in Fond du Lac, the Garroway Museum and the Octagon House which Edwin helped his father Isaac build in 1856, and the lighthouse on the edge the lake, our triumvirate's official headquarters. There, sheltered from the breeze coming off the lake, we hold our annual meeting.

"Here ye, here ye, I call our membership to order," says Grandma.

"I second the motion," I say.

"Me too," says Lenore. "Any new business?"

"I propose that we meet here again next summer."

"I second the motion," says Lenore.

"Sold," says Grandma.

"Is that it?" I ask.

"I have one other piece of business," says Grandma.

"Yes sir."

"I propose that any stone erected for me at the cemetery state that I am the daughter of Flora Powers Brown."

Perfect. It's perfect. There is no marker for Flora in Oregon. There should be one here, in the town of her birth. There should be something somewhere that says she existed, for if it were not for Flora, we would not be here, shivering in the wind at the lighthouse on the edge of the lake. We would not exist at all.

"I second the motion," says Lenore.

"I third it," I say.

And it is done.

"May I make a suggestion," says Grandma.

Lenore and I nod, shaking.

"I propose we adjourn for hot coffee."

We race to the car, heading to the restaurant down the street from Aunt Nora's house, where Grandma used to listen to her Uncle John roll barrels of hootch across the basement floor. We sit, warming our hands on our mugs, reflecting about the long journey to find each other, and all the adventures we have shared.

"You know," says Grandma, "to me, our triumvirate is much more than just the three of us. It includes all our mothers, all our ancestors."

"A toast then," says Lenore, raising her coffee.

"To our foremothers," I say, and we clink our mugs together. Here's to Cheddar Man's mother, and all of her daughters. "Each and every one."

63

A decade and a half ago, I stood at a pay phone in the San Francisco Airport talking to the oncologist who was treating my mother. Mom knew her cancer was serious, but she didn't know her prognosis yet. I waited until I was alone at the airport before calling her doctor. "Shouldn't she be receiving some kind of aggressive therapy?" I ask.

I was unprepared for his words. "There's no reason to put her through that. She has only a few weeks."

I could barely breathe. A few weeks?

I hung up and immediately tried to call Jon at his office, but he was at a meeting off campus. I lost it then, sobbing uncontrollably, all alone beside the pay phone while strangers walked past, giving me sideways glances on the way to their gates. The airline announced my flight was boarding, but instead of getting in line with the other passengers, I picked up the phone again, my hand shaking as I dialed.

"Hello?" Liz's voice made all the strangers around me disappear. I was no longer alone.

"Liz?" I couldn't keep from breaking into a sob.

"Jeannie? Jesus, what's wrong?"

Our friendship grew from early morning rows in college to selection camps and long letters written from around the world. But on that day in the airport, Liz was much more than a rowing friend. I do not remember what she said to me during that short phone call before I boarded the flight to Massachusetts. I just remember that at that moment, she was my family.

So often, friends have been there, like an ark, keeping me afloat during floods. Like the day Jonathon hemorrhaged following his tonsillectomy and I turned around in the hospital waiting room to find my friend Jean King standing beside me. I hadn't called or asked her to come. Somehow she just knew.

We met while registering our children for school. "What can you tell me about this magnet school with the science program?" she'd asked the district clerk behind the counter, and I jumped from my place in line to tell her about Tiff's experience at the school. It turned out this stranger lived only a block from me. "What's your name?" she asked.

"Jean."

"You're joking," she said, taking my hand. "So's mine." It turned out her husband's name was also John and that her two sons were nearly the same ages as Tiff and Jonathon. So we became friends, Jean and Jon and Jean and John, spending evenings in front of the fireplace sharing good wine and deep thoughts. But never did our friendship mean more to me than when I turned around at the hospital and there she was.

Sometimes I have been able to reciprocate, to help friends the way they help me. Like the day Beth called me from her parents in Connecticut, frantic because she couldn't find her wedding ring, afraid she'd accidentally thrown it out back at her house. I spent the rainy November afternoon going through every room of the house she and Fred were renovating, and every inch of the twelve foot dumpster outside. Soaking wet, I felt like I'd won the lottery when I found her ring, slightly bent but intact, under a pile of leaves in the street.

Friends have been like family, sharing life with me, encouraging me along the way. "You can do it," they have said when I've faced rejection. "Don't give up. And by the way, there's a piece of broccoli between your teeth." Friends tell me things no one else will. They have helped make me who I am.

It's a rare thing when it happens. Out of all the people I've crossed paths with, only a handful have become friends. They are precious, more valuable than any wealth. I do not lose track of them. Well, except one.

Jackie sends me the obituary. "I thought you'd want to know..."

Jan, my best friend from so long ago, the one who wore jeans and high-tops just like me, the one I spent hours with riding horses over dry grass hills, the one who disappeared from my life, who I haven't seen in three decades: her mother has passed away.

Thirty years. What happened? We'd been best friends, inseparable. Her married name and the town where she lives are listed in the obituary and I pick up a pen and begin to write. "Dear Jan, I'm so sorry to hear about your mom..."

I don't receive a response. Then, months later, the phone rings. "Jeannie? It's Jan."

"Who?"

"Jan," she laughs, and the familiarity of that husky sound, even after all these years, takes me home. Instantly, we pick up right where we left off three decades before, talking non-stop. My old friend grew up to become a horse whisperer and an adoptive parent. When we reunite with Linda, the three of us are confounded. "Why did we drift apart?" We have no answers. All we know is that we won't be parted again.

Jackie smiles when we tell her about our reunion. "You three always did breathe the same air." The same air. Maybe that's it, this magic connection that exists between friends.

Last year, my friend Liz learned she had cancer. She didn't call me sobbing from an airport pay phone. She is much braver than me. She sent me, along with her many other friends, a generic email. 'Hi y'all. I hope you don't mind a general e-broadcast of this... I found out last week that I have cancer...'

Fortunately, her prognosis was excellent. She faced her decisions regarding her illness with both humor and grace, and her large family rallied around her, providing an army of support.

And she has had all of us, too, friends from the many eras and arenas of her life. We've shown up unannounced and taken her out for long breakfasts at the Homemade Café and browsed through Berkeley's bookstores and sat in front of her fireplace, reminiscing and sharing deep thoughts. We've made her laugh. We breathe the same air. We are family.

64

When my dad starred in his high school play, one of his lines was, "I'm not an old man; fifty-two isn't an old man." I discovered the script inside his Santa Barbara High School annual long after he was gone, when scrapbooks and yearbooks were the only way I could know him. "Fifty-two isn't an old man." My dad was fifty-two when he died. That line he uttered in the play was right: he wasn't old.

I watch my sons chasing each other in the backyard. They are close to the age I was when I lost my father and I know if I were to die today, they would not remember much about me. I cannot remember my father's voice. I would not even recognize it if I heard it. Within months of his death, the memory of it escaped, like a bird out a window.

I seem to focus on his death, but I come by it honestly. I grew up in a society that still runs the Zapruder film every November 22nd. It's imprinted. Click, click, click, each frame of Kennedy's assassination rolls through my memory and so do the events of the week when my father died.

The last time I saw him was on a Friday morning, before I left for school. I never considered I wouldn't see him again. If I had, I don't know what I would have done, clung to him perhaps. But it was like any other day. I hugged him goodbye and walked down La Cañada Road to catch the bus, and everything I knew about him in that moment was all I would ever know of him.

I might not remember his voice, but I do remember his smile. I remember the night he helped me build a pinewood derby racing car, even though I wasn't a Cubscout, the two of us painting the car together, the smell of the enamel and the feel of his hand guiding mine on the brush.

The pinewood derby racer sits on a shelf in my office today, every so often catching my eye, giving me pause, making me wish that I knew my father now, that I had more than childhood memories of him.

Dad's best friend in high school and college, Charlie Stevens, wrote in his yearbook, "I'd rather be with you in a football game, fight, play, or whatever, than any other guy in the world." I haven't seen Charlie since Dad's funeral, three decades ago. My Aunt Rena gives me his address.

> *Dear Charlie,*
> *I've been thinking a lot about my dad, and wishing I knew more about him. Do you have any anecdotes from all the years you knew each other that you can share with me?*

When Charlie writes back, I open the envelope to find a single sheet of yellow legal paper inside with just a few words scrawled on it. But his letter tells me everything I really need to know.

> *Dear Jean,*
> *Your father was the best friend I ever had. I can say no more.*

With Mom it is different. I knew her as an adult. I remember her voice clearly. "Belonging to a family has nothing to do with words." So calm. "You want money Frank. Let me tell you where I have some hidden." So honest. "It isn't much, but it's yours, everything the agency was willing to give us."

For months, after her death, I absentmindedly picked up the telephone and dialed her number to tell her something, sometimes not realizing my mistake until the automated message came on telling me her line was disconnected. Then one day a person answered. The telephone company had given Mom's number away and I never called again after that.

But she is never far from my thoughts. I was acutely aware of her absence when the boys learned to walk, to talk, and to tie their shoes. I miss sharing motherhood with her, the little day to day moments, like when Jonathon proclaims, "Wow, the month of July flew by like an acrobat," then pauses and asks, "What's an acrobat?" She is not here to laugh, to enjoy her grandsons. I cannot call her to tell her about the fish tank we got Tiff, about how he carefully selected three goldfish, his first pets, or that within days, the tank got so dirty, we could barely see the fish anymore.

The pet store said, "Buy a couple algae eaters," so we did, but the tank only got dirtier. Finally, I emptied it and scrubbed the sides and refilled the tank with clean water. Now we could see the fish, but the next morning, all five were floating belly-up. The pet store next recommended we get an indestructible Japanese fighting fish instead, so Tiff picked one out and named him "Blue". The very next day I caught Tiff pouring a glass of pink guava juice into Blue's water. No wonder the tank was always so dirty.

Mom would have had a good laugh and patted the side of the fish tank, whispering, "Good luck, Blue." (He actually seemed to thrive on pink juice and lived a good long life.)

So often I have needed her guidance. Like the time I found Jonathon standing beside the open drawer of my night stand, staring at the stack of envelopes hidden inside. He was very familiar with the envelopes and the words scrawled upon them. "Dear tooth fairy. Here is my tooth for one dollar."

Jonathon turned from the envelopes and looked up at me. "You're the tooth fairy?"

I did what perhaps many parents do when confronted with the end of childhood fantasies. I lied. "This is just between you and me," I said, my arm draped confidentially around his shoulder. "I handle the tooth concession for our neighborhood."

"You mean you do this for everybody?"

"Uh, just around here."

"Wow!"

After he left the room, I slapped a hand to my forehead. I had lied to my beautiful, innocent son. What was I thinking? What would Mom say? I struggled to remember how she handled Santa Claus and the tooth fairy and the Easter Bunny and knew only one thing for sure: I was positive Mom never told me she ran the tooth fairy concession for La Cañada Road.

"My mom is the tooth fairy," Jonathon told the other children in his class. Parents remarked about this while we waited outside the school for the release bell to ring. "I hear you're the tooth fairy," one mother said, her arms crossed. "My daughter wants me to tell you she'd like a raise."

My face reddened. My lie had reached geometric proportions. As hundreds of children streamed out of the school, Jonathon ran toward me with his gap-toothed smile and leapt into my arms, provoking a sudden flashback of myself leaping into Mom's arms after school, so long ago. I felt a surreal sensation, as if I was her for a moment, as if I knew exactly how she felt to be my mother.

And I suddenly knew exactly what she would say to me about my being the tooth fairy. Every parent makes mistakes. Learn from them and move on. Don't dwell. And while you're at it, give the girl who wants a raise an extra dime.

I feel my mother inside of me. She will always be a part of my touch, my heart, my soul. When I am at my best as a mother, I am her. I can hear her.

And somewhere deep inside, I can hear my father, too. I cannot tell you how his voice sounds, but it feels like a hand guiding my own upon a paint brush.

65

It began with rowing lessons which grew into a friendship, then something more, something unexpected and wonderful. When we married, starting a family was not on our agenda. Jon and I never even discussed having children. So at two o'clock in the morning on our four-month wedding anniversary, I lay awake in bed, worried. I was pretty sure I was pregnant and had no idea how Jon would react to the news. Being a thoughtful and considerate spouse, I shook him awake. "Honey?"

"Mrph?" He opened one eye and looked at me in the dim nightlight.

"How would you feel if I was pregnant?"

"Hnph?"

"If I was going to have a baby, how would you feel?"

He blinked, rolled over and murmured, "You remember Groucho Marx's television show?"

Groucho Marx? "I think that went off the air before I was born."

He yawned. "Well, whenever someone said the magic word, a duck came down from the ceiling with a hundred dollar bill."

A duck? My mind raced, trying to interpret this. A magic word. A hundred dollar bill. "Does that mean you'd be happy?"

Silence.

"Honey?"

Light snoring.

A duck?

The next day, my doctor said, "I think you're pregnant." He did a test to prove it, promising to call me in the morning with the results. I stopped by a toy store, bought a small stuffed duck, sewed a Monopoly hundred dollar bill to it's wing, and dangled it from the rearview mirror when I picked up Jon from work.

He slid into the passenger seat and squinted at the duck. "What's this?"

"You know." I grinned. "The magic word."

He squinted harder. "Magic word?"

"Remember? Groucho Marx. The duck that came down from the ceiling with a hundred dollar bill."

He shrugged, his expression blank.

Uh oh. "It looks like I might be pregnant."

Jon did not clutch his chest apoplectically, like I feared he might. He said, "Wow," and then he smiled.

It turned out, there was no magic word, I wasn't pregnant. But a year later, I bought one of those home pregnancy test kits, and the stick turned blue. I stitched a real hundred dollar bill to the duck's wing, and this time I didn't have to explain the significance of it dangling from the rearview mirror when I picked up Jon at work.

I worried the whole time I was pregnant. Books I read suggested I should be experiencing a bond with the baby growing inside, but I felt no particular affection toward my abdomen as it stretched to Jabba the Hutt proportions. I worried that this lack of bonding meant I wouldn't be a good mother.

The labor lasted thirty hours. When the pains intensified, Jon was asleep in a chair near my hospital bed, so I threw a pillow at him and yelled for some Demerol. At that point, I didn't care if I had a boy or a girl or a squid, and I worried that this attitude probably indicated I would not be a good mother.

It happened in an instant, a final push, a single intake of air, and the worst pain I ever felt in my life disappeared, replaced by a much more powerful feeling.

"It's a boy."

Jon placed our son, Tiff, in my arms and I was forever changed. I had become a mother. I no longer worried about whether or not I would be a good one, I was too worried about other things, bilirubin counts, teething, tiny sneezes and strained peas. When I got pregnant again a year later, I dusted off the duck and the hundred dollar bill and picked up Jon at his office. I worried the entire time I was pregnant, afraid that I would never be able to love another child as much as Tiff.

The labor was long. When the pains intensified, Jon was reading the "Wall Street Journal" in a chair across the room so I threw a pillow at him and yelled for some Demerol.

Jonathon was born a few hours later and when I looked into his eyes, I was forever changed. I became his mother, too.

At night, I sit in the rocking chair in their room, watching their chests rise and fall, worried that if I leave, they might forget how to breathe. When I finally go to bed, I turn up the volume on the intercom on my nightstand. Suddenly, I hear a noise: a loud giggle, followed by a snicker. My sons are laughing at my neuroses already.

I try hard to be a good mother. I take the boys for walks in the park, feed them regularly, attend to their every need, sing them songs and read them *Good Night Moon* and teach them how to say "please" and "thank you."

I make the mistake of boasting about being a good mother once, during a lunch for the trustee wives of the college, when I say, "Mothers are much better at parenting than fathers." To illustrate my point, I relate a recent incident.

Jon was supposed to be watching Tiff, but engrossed in the Sunday paper, he'd lost track of him. Searching the house, he finally found our son seated inside the toilet upstairs, happily splashing water as if he were in a wading pool. While the other women at the table laugh, I state emphatically that such a thing would never occur on my watch.

Two of the wives ask if they can stop by my house later to see the baby. When the doorbell rings, I hurry downstairs, realizing I have no idea where Tiff is. As I approach the front door, I see him, inside the downstairs bathroom, sitting in the toilet, happily splashing: my son, the future Olympic swimmer, or perhaps, plumber. I answer the door with a soaking wet kid in my arms and never brag about being a good mother again.

Tiff and Jonathon are my spiritual advisors. They teach me things about the world I would otherwise never notice. They even teach me about myself.

Jonathon is waking from his nap, and as Tiff races ahead of me into their bedroom, he closes the door behind him and locks it, giggling. I wait a moment or two, then tap on the door. "Come on, Tiff. Unlock the door."

The giggling intensifies, but I hear Tiff trying to comply with my request. He spins the bolt part way, but the eighty-year-old lock is stiff, and after several unsuccessful attempts at twisting the bolt open, Tiff whimpers. "I can't do it."

There are no keys for these old doors. "Hang on Tiff," I say, and run to the room next door. From the window, it would be a six foot leap to reach the boys' room. If I should miss, it is fifteen feet to the ground.

Tiff begins to sob, and Jonathon joins him. There's only one thing to do, a thing that a confirmed acrophobic hates: I have to go 'up.'

I grab the cherry-picking ladder from the garage and rush to the side of the house, lean it against the wall, and call to my frightened sons, "I'm coming boys!"

It has rained all week and the ground is soft. I take one step and the ladder falls over. I plant it again, and step onto the first rung, then the second. Very, very slowly, I inch my way up, terrified at being eight feet high, then ten, then twelve, my arms and legs shaking.

From the sound of it, Tiff and Jonathon are equally terrified at being locked inside a room. Their cries spur me higher and higher, until I reached the window, fifteen feet up. They can see me, just outside and cry in unison. "Mom-my!"

The screen won't budge, so I break it and slide the unlocked window open. Shifting my weight over the window sill, I push off against the top rung and the ladder falls backward, landing in the rhododendrons. I hang, half in, half out the window, my feet spinning like an egg-beater against the outer wall of the house, trying to push myself inside. Tiff stops crying, watching the proceedings with interest.

With a final effort, I push forward and fall into their room. "Wow!" Tiff exclaims as I sprawl on the floor, and Jonathon starts to laugh. I hug them both, then look out the window at the ladder on the ground below.

I am terrified of heights. I have always said that I couldn't climb a ladder if my life depended on it. But this wasn't about my life. This was about my sons.

It began because of rowing lessons, and became something more, something unexpected and wonderful: a family. And nothing I ever put on any family tree will be as important as the names of my sons.

Ever.

66

What is family?

Unlike the blank sheet of manilla paper I felt so uncomfortable facing in the third grade, today I confidently face a large blank canvas and paint the names on it, one by one. My brothers and sisters; Lenore; Mary; Ed and Flora; Edwin and Ruth; Thomas and Hannah Brown; Jabez and Rachael Arnold; row by row I paint my ancestors onto my family tree, all the way back to Elizabeth Tilley and John Howland who traveled to America aboard the Mayflower, and beyond.

The first royalty I can include are Ynir, the King of Gwentland in the twelfth century, and his wife Nesta, the Princess of Glamorgan. They are my twenty-seventh great grandparents. Say "great" twenty-seven times, go back thirty couples, and that is how we are connected.

When I initially learned about them, I was impressed. I descend from royals! Then I did the math. I have (for that matter, everyone has) *536,817,912* twenty-seventh great grandparents. That's over half a billion people, more people than lived on the entire planet when Ynir and Nesta were breathing. It was the moment I realized: I am related to everybody.

Hello cousin.

I can reach back even further into the past, all the way to Christmas Day in the year 800 when my forty-second great grandfather, Charlemagne, was crowned the Holy Roman Emperor. He was already the King of France. Of course, before I go shouting from the treetops that I descend from Charlemagne, it's important to point out that it isn't hard to find one of his descendants. Pretty much, anybody can get to know one by looking in the mirror.

I know now that the little speck that was me in the third grade has millions of ancestors, some noteworthy, some heroic, some average hardworking souls, some whose names are lost to posterity, and others whose names are notorious. They are a part of me, a part of us all. I walk down any street and smile at my newfound cousins, which is basically everyone I encounter.

I am a griot, a keeper of history. As I paint the names of these ancestors on my family tree, I reflect on how their actions, large and small, affected the course of families, of history. Their stories have taught me that what we do in life impacts our descendants. Our names may not be remembered for long, but our deeds set in motion all that follows.

This is immortality: the time we spend with our children, our random acts in our communities, be they kind or unkind. My quest for a family tree has taught me this, and it has also made me realize something important: we are all connected. I have heard this all my life, but I never *felt* it until now.

The long journey has brought me back home, to my mom, to Betty. Her ancestors may not be directly my own, but the day the social worker put me in her arms, my mother became a part of my family tree. Her strength and nurturing are her legacy to me and my children and all who follow.

It isn't until I'm painting the family tree that I can see my error, that my conception of family has been wrong all along. There are others who belong on it. I draw light pencil lines on the canvas above my name just like my teacher taught me to do in the third grade.

There is no more research I need to do, no more records I need to unearth. I have always known these names: Giuseppe Sacconaghi. Maria Soldavini. Effie Brumbaugh. Stanley Wenger. I add them to my chart along with my parents, Betty and Lou. I have known them my whole life, but I never understood before that they belonged to me, that they, too, are part of my family tree. They helped make me who I am.

Friends belong on the tree, as well. They have believed in me when I didn't believe in myself, been there for me in the dark, celebrated with me in the sun, and will be there for my children when I am gone. They are part of my family, too.

There isn't room for everyone. My small canvas holds only seven hundred names, seven hundred stories.

I am finally done. Mrs. Stadleman would be proud. She would put a gold star on my family tree and I would take it home where it belongs, and put it on my wall.

I am like Dorothy in *The Wizard of Oz*. I have had the power within me, always, to create this portrait of my family, but I needed to make this journey in order to understand what I have always known inside. I can click my heels together now and say the words. "There's no place like home, there's no place like home..."

I am back, and like Dorothy, I never really left. Like Dorothy, my family has been with me throughout my odyssey: my husband and my sons; my mom and dad; my grandparents and cousins and aunts and uncles; my friends; my birth family; my ancestors. They are all holding hands together in a huge circle, dancing within me. They are my family.

And yours.

My Family Tree

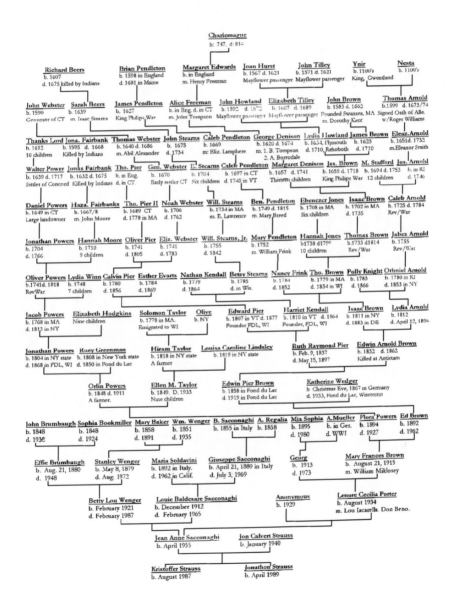

It has been forty-five years since Lenore walked out the doors of the county hospital with a social worker three days after she gave birth to me. She did not want to come back. "I hate Martinez. It's an ugly place."

"But you were here during the early spring when it's green and beautiful."

"Martinez is not beautiful." Her words are firm.

As we turn off the highway, I can see a tall building in the distance, and as we draw closer, Lenore points. "There it is!" The low, single story building is dwarfed by the brand new hospital behind it.

Together, we walk through the double doors into the old lobby. Flourescent light does not brighten the drab yellow walls.

"I remember this," Lenore breathes. "I remember."

No one stops us as I follow her down the cement corridor to a second set of double doors. A heavy padlock signals we have gotten as far as we are going to get. "This is it," says Lenore. "I'm sure of it." She flags down a man wearing a hospital I.D. "Excuse me, is this the maternity ward?"

"Maternity's on the fourth floor of the new building," the man says, jerking his thumb toward the shiny new hospital.

"But is this where babies were born in 1955?"

"Lady, do I look like I'm old enough to have been working here that long?"

Lenore stops the next person, a nurse, and asks again, and the nurse nods. "Yes, this used to be maternity."

"I knew it!" The two of us stand on tiptoe, peering through the window in one of the doors. There is stuff all over the floor, ceiling tiles, old equipment and debris. Maternity is being dismantled. Back in the drab lobby, Lenore appeals to the receptionist. "Is there any chance we can get into that locked wing?"

"Absolutely not," says the woman.

Lenore and I share a grin. We have encountered a gatekeeper. We have encountered a lot of gatekeepers.

I don't want to cause any trouble. "It's okay," I tell Lenore. "I've seen enough."

"No," she insists. "I want to walk down that corridor with you."

An orderly walks past and whispers, "Try physical plant. Extension 5240."

Lenore picks up a phone and dials the number. "Hello? This is Lenore Beno, from Minnesota. I'm here with my daughter and I need you to unlock the old maternity ward in the original hospital building so I can show her where she was born."

I almost burst into laughter. I'm sure whoever is on the phone isn't going to care what the heck Lenore Beno from Minnesota wants, but to my surprise the man on the other end of the line says, "I'll be right down." Five minutes later he arrives, a large ring of keys clinking at his side, removes the padlock, and leaves us alone in the dimly lit corridor.

I kneel down and touch the floor. My birth mother was wheeled across these worn linoleum tiles nearly half-a-century ago. She has told me she felt many things that day. She felt beneath everyone. She was a fallen woman, a woman who was about to lose her first child.

She walks ahead of me now, her head held high, as I linger behind, pausing in front of the small room with darkened windows and the door marked Nursery, *pressing my nose against the dusty glass. This is where I spent my first three days.*

"Jean."

I look up and see Lenore waving for me to join her at the end of the hallway and I'm surprised by her megawatt smile. "I was going to ask if you were doing okay," I say, "but you look fine."

"Fine? I'm great!" She'd been so nervous about coming here, yet she's grinning this goofy grin. "Look!" She points at the large wooden door.

DELIVERY ROOM 1
KEEP DOORS CLOSED

Together, we push open the heavy door and walk inside. Except for ceiling tiles scattered on the floor, the room is bright and clean. I flick a switch on the wall and the huge round lights above the delivery theater illuminate the room. "Wow!" I take a picture of my birth mother there, under the lights, and she takes one of me, standing in the exact spot where I was born, my arms outstretched.

"This," says Lenore, "is a remarkable day."

Earlier, we had gone to the county adoption agency which handled my placement. We carried with us a copy of <u>Birthright</u>. In all the years since I had written the book, I had never once shared any insights about my reunion with the social workers there. I was not sure how they would feel about an adoptee barging into their office with a book extolling the virtues of being reunited.

Lenore and I sat outside the county building in my car for a long time. She was feeling very much like the 'tainted woman' she'd been labeled as long ago. "We don't have to do this," I said. "The last thing I want is for you to feel uncomfortable."

Finally, we decided to see if we could just give the book to a staff member, but when we entered the packed lobby, my heart sank. There were so many people waiting, and we hadn't made an appointment or anything. I explained to the receptionist that I was adopted through this agency long ago, and I just wanted to drop off this book. I introduced Lenore.

"I'll let one of the social workers know you're here," the young woman said. "But as you can see, we're very busy." She picked up the phone and turned her back to us. After a few moments, she hung up and said, "Someone will be out in a few minutes to take your book, but I have to ask you to wait out there, by that door." She pointed out to the entryway.

We weren't even allowed to stay in the lobby? "Do you want to just leave?" I asked Lenore as we exited.

She shook her head. "We should make sure they get a copy of your book."

Barely a minute passed when the door opened and a very pleasant-looking woman came out. "Hello." She held out her hand. "I'm the supervisor of this unit. I'm so excited you've come."

Lenore and I looked at each other. Excited?

"Do you have a moment to come inside? Please. It would mean so much." She held open the door and we followed her.

An astonishing sight greeted us. A dozen social workers gathered in a circle and Lenore and I were brought chairs to sit in. The supervisor touched Lenore's shoulder. "This is one of our mothers," she said gently. The social workers nodded and smiled. Then the supervisor touched my shoulder. "And this is one of our babies."

Their eyes were full of respect, their hearts full of questions, and for nearly an hour, Lenore and I sat and talked about our experiences. It was so unexpected, so wonderful, and I watched my birth mother sitting tall beside me, no longer a fallen woman, but a teacher.

We each take a discarded ceiling tile from the delivery room, then walk back through the corridor to the old lobby. I look around one last time at the yellow walls, at the stern receptionist, at the double doors leading to maternity. They will be gone soon, but I won't need to see them again. I have found the answers I was seeking.

I know where I came from. I know my family. They are the people who raised me and the people whose blood flows in my veins. They are the people I've chosen to share my life with and others who've crossed my path along the way. My family is whoever and whatever I want it to be.

"Thank you for giving birth to me," I say to my mother beside me.

She smiles. "Thank you for being born."

We step arm-in-arm through the threshold of the hospital out to where the rolling hills are green, and the California poppies look like gold in the morning sun.

Harriet and Edward Pier

Lydia Arnold Brown

Ruth Pier

Edwin Arnold Brown

Pier Brown

Mia Sophia

Ed Brown II

Flora Powers

Effie Brumbaugh

Stanley Wenger

Giuseppe Sacconaghi

Maria Soldavini

Betty Wenger and Lou Sacconaghi

Lenore Cecilia Porter

Mary Frances Brown

left to right: (back) Charles, Bobby, Jim, Mike (front) Sue, Cathy, Jean, Mary

Jon

Jean

Tiff

Jonathon

List of Illustrations

Many photos are from Jean Strauss's private collection. Others have come from the following organizations and individuals.

Harriet and Edward Pier	Fond du Lac Public Library
Lydia Arnold Brown	Fond du Lac Historical Society
Ruth Pier	Fond du Lac Historical Society
Edwin Arnold Brown	Craig Johnson
Pier and Ed Brown, Flora Powers, Mia Mueller	Caroline Leckel
Maria Soldavini	Rena Sacconaghi Black
Lenore Cecilia Porter	Don Beno
Mary Frances Brown	Lynn High

Libraries and Research Centers

Numerous libraries (and librarians) assisted in providing information, in particular:

The American Antiquarian Society, Worcester, Massachusetts

Antietam National Battlefield, Sharpsburg, Maryland

Blanding Public Library, Rehoboth, Massachusetts

Church of Latter Day Saints, Genealogy Library, Maryland and California

D.A.R. Library, Washington, D.C.

Fond du Lac Historical Society, Fond du Lac, Wisconsin

New Berlin Library, New Berlin, New York

New England Genealogical Historical Society

New York Public Library, New York, New York

Norwich Library, Norwich, New York

Old Colony Historical Society, Taunton, Massachusetts

Plimoth Plantation, Plymouth, Massachusetts

Rhode Island Historical Society, Providence, Rhode Island

Wisconsin State Historical Society, Madison, Wisconsin

Bibliography

Of the numerous books and other resources used in the course of writing this book, a handful have been directly cited and others have provided valuable information relayed herein.

Little House in the Big Woods, Laura Ingalls Wilder, © 1932, HarperCollins.

Roots, Alex Haley, © 1976, Doubleday.

The Wonderful Wizard of Oz, L. Frank Baum, © 1899

The Sixth Wisconsin Volunteers, Rufus Dawes, © 1890, Morningside Press.

The Portrait of an American, Bascom N. Timmons, © 1953, Henry Holt.

Colonial History, edited by Stanley Katz, © 1976, Little, Brown & Co., Inc.

Of Plymouth Plantation 1620-1647, William Bradford, © Knopf, 1994.

Flintlock and Tomahawk, Douglas Edward Leach, © 1958, Parnussus.

The Patriot Chiefs, Alvin M. Josephy, Jr., © 1958, Penguin Books.

The Iron Brigade, by Alan Nolan,© 1961, 1994, Indiana University Press.

How I Escaped the Red Guns, Mia Mueller, © 1954, Clear Thoughts Pub.

Denison Genealogy, Denison, Peck and Jacobus, © 1963, Pequot Press.

New England Historical and Genealogical Register, Vol. XXXIII, © 1879.

John Browne, Gentleman of Plymouth, George Tilden Brown, © 1919, R.I.

Personal Papers, James Brown, courtesy of Beverly Brown

The Sacconaghi Family Genealogy, compiled by Valerie Giorgi, 1987.

The Wenger Family Genealogy, © 1971.

Fond du Lac Centennial Program, © 1936.

The Life and Writings of Jerome A. Watrous, © 1992, William H. Washburn.

In the Bloody Railroad Cut at Gettysburg, L. Herdegen & W. Beaudot, © 1990

Benny Havens, Oh!, a West Point Cadet song. Published in Buffalo, NY.

ACKNOWLEDGMENTS

My parents, Betty and Lou Sacconaghi, have been the inspiration for much of my writing. I only wish they had lived long enough to know their grandchildren and to have been able to pass on more of the special qualitites that they both possessed. My mom was a remarkable parent. I am now the same age she was when she became a widow and my middle-aged perspective makes me all the more in awe of her ability to provide me a stable home in the midst of the chaos of my brother's illness. She is my hero. My dad was the photographer of the family. I have only five photographs of the two of us together. One is on the cover of this book, where he is only a shadow. That's how I see him in my life. He is gone, but his presence is with me, always.

I was blessed not only to have been raised by them, but to have been supported through the years by my Sacconaghi relatives, Rena, Jim, and Larry Black, Connie, Mickey and Jim Martin, and my Wenger relatives: Ruth, Dick and Fred Gray; Bernice, Walter, Joyce and Tom Stebbins; Marty, Jim, Dave, and Kathleen Garber; and Dorothy Baker. They have been, and will always be, my family.

My birthmother, Lee, and my grandmother, Mary, always encouraged me to, "Just do it!" Much of this book grew out of adventures we have shared and difficult experiences we have gone through together. These two 'tall' women have illuminated my life in so many ways. I will love them forever.

My birth family has indulged me over the years as I have shared our story: Mary and Kelly, Mike and Vicky, Sue and Kevin, Jim and Cheryl, Cathy, Bob and Christi, and Charles; my nephews and nieces, Jeremiah, Jennifer, Joseph, Veronica, Luke, Justin, Madesyn, Chase, Taylor, Collin, Reed, Lucas, and Maximo; Lee's husband, Don; as well as Christina Jackson, and Bill and Tom Miklosey. We are bound now, not only by blood, but by the times we have shared together. I will be forever grateful that we found each other.

A handful of people have mentored me, beginning with Bruce Reeves, whose enthusiasm for this story and skill as an editor, were a driving force behind getting this down on paper. Jameson and Darleen Parker have sustained me with witty emails on days when flipping burgers seemed like a reasonable career change. Friends read through portions of this manuscript (some more than once!) helping me in countless ways. My eternal gratitude to Charmian Carr, Barbara Drapos, Lynn Franklin, Lue Jones, Jean King, John Riley, Margaret Russell, Kim Sandmann, and Jan Gaeta Watterson.

Others have helped me in equally important ways: Joel Cinnamon on the cover design; my sons' godparents, Kathryn Forte and Lee Blackman, Kathy Long Phinney and Duane Hickling; the Five Club of Kaja Weeks, Rhonda Giles, Susie Ostermeyer and Patty Levillain, who provided late night encouragement as well as handwriting analysis; Worcester friends, particularly the Fray family, the Drapos family, Polly and Dick Traina, and Larry Abramoff; Ellen Dunlop and Jim Moran, and all the librarians of the American Antiquarian Society; Kathy Hill and Beth Borchelt; Susie, John, and Robin Reardon; my 'adoption mentors', Annette Baran, Martha Hulbert, B.J. Lifton and Susan Darke; Mary Hitselberger of the Fond du Lac DAR; John Ebert and Sally Powers of the Fond du Lac Historical Society; newfound cousins, Caroline Leckel and Jim Brown, and my second cousins, Tom Kuchenburg and Ellen Vucovik; Edith Wagner of Reunions Magazine; Mary Jensen of the Contra Costa County Adoption Services Unit; the incredibly generous Craig Johnson; Jon's daughters, Stephanie and Sue, and their families; and my extended family of Liz Miles, Patty Brink, Pat Spratlen, Joy Stockton, Val McClain, Kate Murphy, Robin Spencer, Margie Cate, Jennifer Hunsaker, and Linda and Jackie Warden.

Finally, this book would never have been possible without the love and encouragement of my family. My sons, Tiff and Jonathon, have not only been my biggest cheerleaders, they have also taught me a great deal about family and roots and what life is really all about.

And above all, my ability to tell this story has been, in ways impossible to quantify, largely due to my husband Jon, who has been my friend and staunch supporter every single day. Over the years, he has made it possible for me to not only write, but to grow. Jon, and the family we have made together, are what make the journey all worthwhile.

Other Books by Jean Strauss

The Great Adoptee Search Book
Castle Rock Publishing, 1990.

Birthright: The Guide to Search and Reunion
Penguin Books, 1994.

Forever Liesl: A Memoir of The Sound of Music
With Charmian Carr.
Viking Books, 2000.
NYTimes bestseller.

Letters to Liesl
With Charmian Carr.
Areté Publishing Company, 2001.

Quick Order Form

Fax orders: 909-625-1040. Copy and send this form.

Email orders: www.arete-usa.com

Postal orders: Areté Publishing Company of America

                  P.O. Box 127, Claremont, CA 91711 USA

Beneath a Tall Tree	$15.00 US	$22.50 CAN
Letters to Liesl	$15.00 US	$22.50 CAN

Title(s) of books to ship: _____

_____

Number of books to ship:_____

Name: _____

Address: _____

_____

City: _____ State_____ Zip_____-_____

Telephone:_____

Email:_____

Sales tax: Add 8% tax for products shipped within California.

Shipping:
USA: $5 for the first book and $2 for each additional copy. All books shipped US Priority Mail.
International: $12 for the first book and $4 for each additional copy.

Payment: Check   Credit card

      Visa   MasterCard   AMEX   Discover

Card number:_____

Name on card:_____ **Exp. Date:**___/___

The Triumvirate